HACK THE BIRD

ADVANCED TWITTER PLAYBOOK

ADAM KHAN
@Khanoisseur

For my loving parents and brothers without whose support

About the Author

Adam Khan advises global brands, startups, entrepreneurs, and purpose-driven organizations on strategy, expansion digital transformation, social media marketing, and culture.

He teaches an advanced Twitter Boot Camp, customized for each consulting engagement, sharing valuable, counterintuitive lessons and research, which formed the basis of this book. Techniques contained in this manual have since been used at Fortune 500 companies, startups, and creative agencies, to build loyal and engaged customer bases.

On Twitter, Adam is at @Khanoisseur

.

Adam Khan @Khanoisseur · 3 Mar 2015

The **tweet** that **made** a **billionaire** out of **Uber's first hire.**

travis kalanick @travisk   1/5/10

Looking 4 entrepreneurial product mgr/biz-
dev killer 4 a location based service.. pre-
launch, BIG equity, big peeps involved--
ANY TIPS??

👤 You follow this user

Ryan Graves
@ryangraves

@KonaTbone heres a tip. email me :)
graves.ryan[at]gmail.com

🌐 Translate from Slovak

1/5/10, 8:17 PM

💬 27   🔁 480   🤍 604   ᶴᴵᴵ

Twitter exchange between Uber (ride hail app) founder Travis Kalanick
and Ryan Graves, which led to Graves getting hired by Uber, and later
becoming a billionaire.

May you write your own Twitter success story.

Key Things you'll Learn

1. You get <u>10 seconds and the first four tweets</u> on your Timeline to convince someone to Follow you. How to optimize your Bio and Timeline for these critical 10 seconds, and convert first-time Visitors into Followers.

2. How obeying this <u>70-30 Rule</u> increases your odds of being Followed and getting more engagement from your Tweets.

3. The game plan <u>for your first 100,000 Followers</u>.

4. <u>How to convert Targets</u> (people you want to Follow you) into Followers.

5. <u>The counterintuitive Tweeting frequency to attract Followers</u>.

6. <u>Why the aesthetic of a Tweet</u> determines whether it gets Retweeted.

7. This 100-1 Rule <u>will get you more Followers than Tweeting</u>.

8. <u>How to phrase your Replies</u> for more Retweets.

9. Strategic use of "<u>Digital Pokes</u>" to get people to visit your Timeline.

10. <u>How to Retweet yourself</u>, bump/refresh old Tweets, and get multiple Tweets Retweeted with a single Retweet.

Introduction

In 2013, my biggest struggle in life, somehow, became Twitter. I bought and read every book available on the topic of mastering what is arguably the most difficult social network to break into, but the books failed me. Some of the worst advice I came across:

- Use hashtags in your bio
- Tweet frequently
- Participate vigorously in chats and live tweet conferences

Even Twitter's official tips were pretty basic and vague, often directing you to buy ads to gain more exposure.

Frustrated yet determined, I ditched the expert advice, and began to run hundreds of crazy Twitter experiments (like altering my sleep cycle to get people that lived in different time zones to Follow me), spanning three years and several thousand hours.

The more time that I spent on Twitter, the more it became obvious why the books didn't help. Almost a decade after Twitter launched, there still doesn't exist a definitive "How to Crush it on Twitter" guide. So I decided to share my research (5000+ hours so far).

I'll spare you the gory details of how I uncovered all the things that I did, but I'll say this: Twitter is full of quirks, angles, and nuances, as you'll see shortly—and while some of what I'm about to reveal might make your head spin, I hope you'll come to appreciate the beauty and utility of every single feature of Twitter (Retweet, Like, Direct Message, Timeline, Reply, Lists, etc.), and use these more strategically to achieve both Follower and Engagement growth.

Armed with this knowledge, you can pursue any purpose, from building an audience for your next great idea, to driving more traffic to your blog, to attracting the attention of journalists, policy makers, VCs, to landing that dream job. (Maybe you'll end up documenting your own Twitter adventures and successes in a book.)

I didn't want HACK the BIRD to become a 200-page effort (it's not), because I know few of us have that kind of patience. The writing style is deliberately casual--you won't find lofty prose here because I want everyone—even those who don't speak English as a first language--to be able to understand the most complex Twitter hacks I've outlined.

My Twitter journey has been eye opening on many levels, and while a part of me wishes that my early Twitter self knew what I know now, I do look back with a certain fondness at the hours I spent cranky and confused.

Which brings me to the main reason I wrote this book—I want to save some of you the frustration that comes with Tweeting, that feeling that you're talking to an empty room, and get a head start on making the impact that you really wanted to, when you first joined Twitter.

How does Twitter work?

So let's get down to the two key questions you all probably want answered—the reason you're flipping through HACK the BIRD:

How to get people to Follow you?
How to get people to share your content?

If I had to break down how growth on Twitter works, that list would look something like this:

1. Produce great content.
2. Get this content in front of the right people.
3. Compel these people to share it with their audience so you get new Followers.
4. Reward people that share your content.
5. Continually engage with your community to retain them as Followers.

Ok, that's the general approach, but as you probably know, if you've spent any time on Twitter, or on blogging for that matter, there's a lot more to it than meets the eye. There are numerous "hows" associated with each of the steps above, and answering those requires a firm grasp of the underlying psychology of why people Follow, what makes them Retweet, and why they remain a Follower.

First, if you're not familiar with how content gets shared on Twitter—i.e. not familiar with terms like Retweets (RTs), Quoted Tweets, Likes, Replies and Mentions, I suggest you check out Twitter's Online Help), but the key takeaway is that any time your Tweet is shared, referenced, or liked in the form of a Retweet, Quoted Tweet, Reply, Mention or a Like, you're getting exposure on Twitter.

When people who don't know visit your Twitter, here are the key actions they can perform:

1. Retweet/Quote one or more Tweets from your Timeline (including a Tweet that you Retweeted).
2. Follow you.
3. Reply to one or more Tweets, or Mention you.
4. Like one or more Tweets.
5. Add you to a List.
6. Share your Tweet in an email or on other social media
7. Do nothing.
8. Block you.
9. Mute you.

From your perspective, 1, 2, and 3 would be ideal "conversions"-- especially if the people you convert into Followers are influential, generous Retweeters, and have a large and engaged community. But 4, 5, and 6 are also helpful (5 could indicates they intend to Follow your Tweets indirectly without Following you directly).

(Note, in order for you to be alerted that actions 1-5 have occurred, you'd need to have Notifications turned on, so do that now—see the chapter on Notifications.)

Most savvy/power users will make the decision to Follow you within thirty seconds of seeing your Twitter account, provided you pass the first ten-second test--ten seconds spent quickly glancing at your Bio, Follower/Following Stats, Profile picture, and the first four Tweets on your Timeline (henceforth referred to as the "First Four Tweets")— these are the four most recent/latest Tweets that you posted. At the ten-second mark, they either bounce, or spend another twenty seconds taking a deeper look.

Why are the First Four Tweets so important? 80% of Twitter's traffic comes from mobile, and on Twitter's mobile app and mobile site, people who scroll down your Timeline see four Tweets before Twitter inserts the "Who to Follow" box (recommended other Twitter accounts to Follow). This is where you lose most people because when they get to this point, they have either stopped scrolling down your Timeline, or clicked away to one of the accounts listed in the "Who to Follow". So you get four, "above the fold" Tweets to impress someone into Following you.

Simply put, if you want a first time visitor, especially experienced Twitter users, to Follow you here's what you have to communicate in those ten seconds:

1. You are a real human—a reputable person with an engaged Twitter Following—and not a link and hashtag spamming bot.
2. You provide unique, entertaining, and thoughtful perspectives on a range of issues, and are not too chatty, frivolous, snarky, mean, sexist and racist.
3. If they Follow you, you will get them more exposure by Retweeting, or otherwise will help them with their career, business or mission.
4. You don't Follow people for the sake of gaining more Followers, but that you actually engage with others in a meaningful manner.

So how do you quickly and emphatically convey these points? Read on.

But first, a quick warning:

Don't fake it till you make it

While you may be tempted to buy Twitter Followers—and many people do this to bolster their Follower count, under the mistaken assumption that having a lot of Followers is what lures more Followers—remember that bought Followers are bots, not real people. They do not engage with you like actual humans, and Twitter shuts these accounts down regularly. If you buy Followers, and Twitter takes them away, your real Followers will notice the drop in Follower count, and your real human Followers may lose respect for you, and stop engaging with you.

Also, experienced Twitter users typically check out your list of Followers, and most can spot the fake ones (I'll show you how to identify fake Followers in a subsequent chapter). Would people still

Follow you if they notice you've bought Followers? Maybe, but they'd likely not forget that you did.

Success on Twitter is a slower, more real process--and the approach I'm about to outline is going to help take much of that pain away.

Your Twitter Philosophy—what should you Tweet about?

One of the most important things that you should to try to figure out is your Twitter philosophy. What are you going to Tweet about, and why? I say 'try to' because no one really fully figures out their Twitter end game or mission. Mine is constantly evolving. Yours will too.

When I first started Tweeting in 2012, my Tweets were—and this is being charitable--bland. I was recycling news articles and sharing links about business-related topics. Which made sense at the time, as I did not want any controversial Tweets to hurt potential career opportunities. But that really didn't work out well, in terms of gaining Twitter Followers or engagement from the audience. And this was frustrating--I didn't understand why some people that shared news articles and professional content on Twitter did better while others did not.

In 2014, I started to post photos that I took during my walks around New York City. Documenting my days in pictures, similar to how some people use Snapchat and Instagram, proved to be a surprising hit—Twitter accounts that were enthusiastic about NYC photos and New York-based brands and businesses started following me and sharing my content. As these Tweets also contained unique and original pictures, the reaction was positive, reinforcing my belief that original content, especially in visual form, works really well on Twitter.

Towards the end of 2014, I started to develop a more confident voice, and began to Tweet about things that reflected my broad range of interests, using visuals in more than 50% of my Tweets, infusing humor wherever it was appropriate. Humor does well on Twitter. Sharing your vulnerabilities is actually a good way to build deeper relationships with your Twitter network. And if you're not afraid to show your weird side, you'll be rewarded for your courage.

These days, I largely tweet about social issues, public policy and politics. My earlier fears that this will result in losing followers were largely unfounded, and I actually ended up replacing any followers I may have lost due to the political nature of my tweets with ones who were far more engaged. After the 2016 election, my Tweets became almost exclusively about politics. As word got around that I was sharing political content, covering topics that the mainstream media was ignoring, my follower count went dramatically up.

No one really likes to Follow people that Tweet like bots—relentlessly posting links to news articles will limit your growth. You'll figure out your own Twitter recipe to success—as long as you're not mean, racist, sexist, selfish and pretentious, you'll do fine.

Having said that, it is a good idea to find a few topics or themes that you can focus your content on so you pick up a diverse and influential group of followers. Before I turned political, tweeting about Startups, Venture Capital, Technology, Policy, Photography, Travel, Urban Planning, Health, and History helped me reach people with a broader range of interests, and kept me from running out of content to share. More importantly, once you settle on a handful of themes, you'll be able to target your Tweets at the people most likely to share them, using audience segmentation Lists.

The Timeline Test

As I noted earlier, you get ten seconds to convince a non-Follower or a first time visitor that lands on your Twitter to take a deeper look.

For the vast majority of your Twitter viewers on mobile, having four kickass Tweets "above the fold"—i.e., above the "Who to Follow," box can mean the difference between winning and losing a potential Follower. But it gets a bit more nuanced, as I'll cover in subsequent pages. To set that up, let me walk you through what picky Twitter users (like me) look at when debating whether to Follow someone. I'm also including some guidance that you should consider when shaping your own Twitter profile.

1. Bio Section: This is often the first thing most people look at. In particular:

    a. Twitter handle: Is it memorable? I'm less likely to Follow someone with numbers in their handle: @johnsmith223 or @bondguy007 isn't the best way to brand yourself. Besides, a lot of fake Twitter accounts and bots use numbers in their handle, so avoid numbers in your handle, or risk being mistaken for a bot. Note, Twitter's mobile app only displays your Twitter handle in a mobile notification ("@pmarca Liked your Tweet"), and not your full name, so if you want to get someone's attention, a memorable or intuitive handle works best. Some journalists use the name of their publication in their Twitter handle (BuzzFeed's Ben Smith's handle is @BuzzFeedBen), however, this is problematic when you switch employers and need to change your handle. If you're Verified (indicated by the blue badge on their profile), and change your Twitter handle, you'll lose the Verfied status, until Twitter re-verifies you, as happened with Maggie Haberman from Politico, when she changed her handle from @MaggiePolitico to @MaggieNYT as a result of her move to the New York Times. Worse, when you change Twitter handles, Tweets containing your old handle will not display your new handle, and anyone clicking on the old handle will not be directed to your new handle.

b. Name: I'm more likely to Follow people that use their real name (with some exceptions for good parody accounts). Don't just use a first or last name, or use a full first name, but an initial for the last name, for example: JohnS. Use of abbreviations, acronyms, and business degrees and certifications in the name is a bit of an eyesore, but useful if you want industry people to instantly recognize you—for example, John Smith, PMP isn't the prettiest looking thing, but if you can selectively and briefly modify the name to include these, especially if you're at a conference. Do not, however, use ALL CAPS for the name.

You can also add your company name to your Twitter name: John Smith, Google. This, however, strikes me as a bit desperate.

Note: Some people (salespeople mostly) will run a Google or LinkedIn search to confirm you are a real person, before they decide to Follow you, so if you want these kinds of people to Follow you, maintain a LinkedIn or Google+ Profile.

c. Bio style and tone: I'm less likely to Follow people that use hashtags and symbols ("#ProjectManager" or "♕ Social Media King") in their bio. Amateurs hashtag their bio, so skip them. The style and tone of the bio is important to me. It shows they put an effort into it. But being overly cute, aggressive, or snarky is a turn off, however.

d. Buzzwords: I tend not to Follow people that use phrases like ninja, guru, junkie, foodie, growth hacker, thought leader, expert, maven in their bio--real experts don't feel the need to describe themselves in this manner.

e. Profile picture/header image: I generally do not Follow eggs (default Twitter profile picture), animal avis, and people that use obscene photos or stock images.

2. Last 20 Tweets—I quickly scroll through their last 20, and build a quick mental picture about them. Are they:

a. Bots: Are they simply Retweeting other accounts?

b. Selfish: Do they Retweet others, or are they simply pushing their own agenda? Related, seeing too many manual RTs and Quoted Retweets in a Timeline is also a turnoff.

c. Engaging: Are they getting Retweets and Likes—if they have thousands of Followers but no engagement, they likely bought their Followers or are failing to engage them.

d. Pests: Are they constantly asking celebrities to Follow them back or Retweet them? Are they Tweeting the same thing at different people (usually pitches to partner up or to Retweet about a cause that's dear to them)?

e. Putting an effort into their Tweets: Are they bringing a unique POV, Tweeting about things that are helpful, mixing it up with personal and business stuff, or are they simply recycling content that I can find somewhere else on Twitter?

f. Too talkative (a Tweet every 5 minutes): Do they use Twitter to chat up others or do they produce original thoughts? Are they only talking to a handful of people (being cliquey)? In which case, I might not Follow them, but add them to a List, and read their Tweets from there (people you add to a List but do not Follow will not show up in your main Newsfeed).

g. Abusing/overusing hashtags? Is every other word in their Tweets hashtagged? Are they pulling in unrelated hashtags to bump their Tweets?

h. Allowing automated tools to Tweet on their behalf (horoscopes, Runkeeper/Fitbit/Nike stats, Thanks to New/Top Followers).

i. Addicted to Meerkat and Persicope: It's okay to see one or two of these in 20 Tweets, but any more and I'm unlikely to Follow you.

j. Cross-posting from Instagram, Facebook or Wordpress: This is a deal breaker for me, as it means they're not actually on Twitter, and will likely not see my Tweets or engage with me.

k. Witty, self-aware, and balanced: I have a thing for smart, funny people, but too much snark gets tedious.

3. Engagement: Next I do some quick math—does the engagement their Tweets are producing sync up with their Follower count? For example, if they have 50,000 Followers but are averaging less than 3 Retweets per Tweet, something is amiss. Likely they bought fake Followers. Or they are failing to engage their audience. On the other hand, if they're getting the exact number of engagement per Tweet—i.e., 26 Retweets and 26 Likes for every Tweet, they've purchased that engagement, and it is from bots, not real people.

4. Following count: Do they Follow lots of people—if they Follow less than 10,000 people, chances of you getting a Follow back are good. However, if someone is Following over 10,000 people, chances of them Following you back are high, but the likelihood of engaging with you is low. In my experience, people who Follow 15K or more people rarely interact meaningfully and regularly—they may as well not Follow you. If I Follow someone who Follows thousands of people and they do not engage with me (Like, Comment or Retweet me), I will un-Follow them and add them to a List, instead.

5. Number of Tweets: How many Tweets have they produced-- 1000 or 100,000? Generally, I try not to Follow someone who has over 40K Tweets (unless they are quality Tweets) because in my experience they tend to, be so chatty their Tweets will clog up my Newsfeed. In this case too, I'd add them to a List until they engage me in a meaningful way. This is an important takeaway—don't get too chatty on Twitter or you might get muted or un-Followed.

6. Number and Recency of Likes: Someone's proclivity to Like (i.e. Like a Tweet) is an important consideration--it tells me they are actively listening to their Followers. The number of times someone has Liked is only shown in the Desktop view--a low number (less than 1000 if they've been active on Twitter for 3+ years) of Likes indicates that they are not likely to Like your Tweets.

While you can't check total number of Likes on your iPhone, you can, however, click on the Likes Tab and get a good idea of the frequency and recency of Likes.

Now this sequence of decision making, before I Follow someone, is more rigorous than when I first started out on Twitter. Back then, the first thing I looked at was their Followers count--if they had thousands of Followers, they must be worthy of a Follow, right? Well, not true, as I learnt somewhat belatedly, after making the mistake of Following people based solely on how many Followers they had. I touched on this earlier—anyone can buy (fake) Twitter Followers—but you can't buy real engagement.

Four years of intensive Twitter use later, the number of Followers is no longer my most important criteria for Following someone. So how many people should you Follow? Using the guidelines above, Follow as many as you can that make your Twitter experience fun and educational. I started out mostly Following Verified accounts, brands and a few friends, and was conscious about capping how many I Followed to a 1000 people. But Twitter actually became more interesting when I began to Follow more people, especially the unverified, low-Follower count folks from a range of professional backgrounds—artists, writers, physicians, comedians—and countries. Today, I Follow over 9000 people—8000 directly and 1000 via Twitter Lists—and my Twitter experience has been better for it. My Timeline now is full opportunities to learn from and participate in a broad range of conversations. Plus, Following lots of people is a good signal to send—lets others know that they stand a chance of being Followed back.

Follow people that you sense are being honest and vulnerable. Those that make you laugh or nod in agreement. Maybe even the weird ones. Some of my Like accounts do not have a lot of Followers. But they have good things to share, and their Tweets often introduce me to other interesting accounts, because they are also active Retweeters. Follow those that are going to be important to your strategic objectives—these could be journalists, VCs, policy makers, teachers, coworkers, and people that work at the company that you want a job at.

And some of the things that I outlined in terms of what I like to see before I Follow people may not apply to you. You may need to Follow people who use professional acronyms or freely indulge in link spam and don't Retweet, because they may be your next boss or client or love interest. So go ahead and Follow them.

The Bio

Since the Twitter bio is often the first thing most people look at (and in many cases it is the only thing that matters before they decide to Follow you), I want to reiterate the importance of not only making the bio memorable, but also recognizing the power that comes from being flexible and strategic in its use. In a bit, I'll outline how you can repeatedly modify the bio, to gain more Followers, but first some key points to remember when crafting the A+ bio:

1. Profile picture: Since the profile picture is something most people look at almost immediately upon coming to your Twitter profile, make sure it is well-lit. The picture doesn't have to be professionally taken, but your face should be clearly visible. Remember to check what the photo looks like on mobile (80% of Twitter's users are on mobile), especially in the smaller thumbnail size (48 by 48 pixels) that Twitter displays in Notifications and Followers/Following lists. And don't flip your profile picture on its side (I had an upside down image a long time ago, but now it's become a bit of a clich).

2. Use a Header picture that reinforces your overall brand—on the desktop site, especially, the Header photo occupies more space than it does on mobile. Use a photo of a famous landmark in your city to demonstrate your connection to it. Get creative with the Header photo, but don't use another photo of yourself as the Header image—it's really not doubling the pleasure!

3. List your current and past job titles, employers, and skills (don't use hashtags!), if those are impressive. While this may seem shallow, people will largely Follow you for where you work/have worked and what you've accomplished. Which is why VCs list their successful investments ("early investor in Uber, Twitter, Etsy" but not their failures!) and why authors list their best sellers.

   Avoid phrases like ninja, guru, junkie, foodie, growth hacker, thought leader, expert, maven, wizard, etc.

4. Tagline: A tagline is sometimes the best way to get people to remember you. Humor works well, as you can see from some of my Like Twitter bios:

a. Marc Andreesen (@pmarca): "Where's the kaboom? There was supposed to be an earth-shattering kaboom!"
b. Liana Maeby (@lianamaeby): "Model/physicist/liar"
c. John Stanton (@dcbigjohn): "DC Bureau Chief of http://Buzzfeed.com, reporter, former bouncer and all around dc bama"
d. Erin Gloria Ryan (@morninggloria): "Managing Editor @Jezebel, ex-writer for @Vh1's @BestWeekEver. Hug averse and mean."

5. Optimize your bio for Twitter's search: Twitter lets people search for other people with specific job titles and skills (writer, teacher, actor), companies, interests, and more. So use phrases that describe your position, include the Twitter handle for your present and past employers, and add your interests (biking, coffee, surfing). Avoid hashtags, however.

6. Pinned Tweet: Only applicable to Twitter's Desktop view, you have the opportunity of pinning a Tweet to the top of your Timeline, and this is the first Tweet most people see if they view your Twitter Profile on a desktop browser. Many people will pin one of their star Tweets (one that got a lot of Retweets, Mentions or a celebrity endorsement) although some will pin a Tweet that highlights a cause or project they want to bring attention to. (We'll talk about the strategic use of a pinned Tweet in a bit).

Always check to see what your Profile Picture, Name, and Handle looks like on mobile (80% of Twitter users access the service on mobile), especially in thumbnail format displayed in the Followers list—ask yourself, "If someone saw me in their Followers list, would they check out my Timeline?"

The High-Converting Twitter Timeline: 70-30 Rule

Do you like hanging out with people who are noisy, chatty, or who talk about themselves all the time? Or with those who only like to have conversations with their clique? Me neither.

That's what some people's Twitter Timelines look like: Every other Tweet is a link to a news article. Or its banal stuff, like automated Tweets to summarize their week on Twitter, fitness tracker updates, Swarm check-ins. Just as annoying, their last 10 Tweets are replies to the same 3 or 4 people.

If you take away one thing from this book, let it be this rule: Never let your own Tweets completely dominate your Timeline. If you want the savvy ones to Follow you, strive to maintain a more balanced, "groomed" Timeline. My 70-30 Rule states that 70% of the Tweets on your Timeline should be your own and 30% should be Retweets ("Native" RTs, not Quoted Tweets, where you insert yourself on to others' Tweets).

The point of this is to signal to anyone casually scrolling through your Tweets in an effort to size you up that:

(a) You're not full of yourself.

(b) If they decided to Follow you, they stand a chance of being Retweeted.

(c) You're not going to flood their Newsfeed with your Tweets (especially automated Tweets).

A Timeline full of your own Tweets, Manual RTs, and Quoted Tweets is not balanced, and implies you are selfish, insecure, or even a Twitter novice, when perhaps you did not know the importance of striking a balance between your own Tweets, and sharing the best content from others.

And while Twitter is about having conversations with your audience (and the 70-30 Rule allows for Replies, as you'll see), getting too chatty, and clogging up your Timeline with an excessive number of consecutive

Replies--unless each and every one these Tweets is in some way remarkable—limits your Twitter growth, and you could actually end up losing Followers with each new Tweet.

Similarly, successive—5 or more--Tweets on your Timeline about your own thoughts and feelings about sports, politics, TV shows and even too many live Tweets from a conference could also deter people from Following you.

I respect people that Retweet others. And I Follow the ones that make an effort to balance their own original thoughts with great Retweets and on-point Replies.

The 70-30 Rule was born after having spent hundreds of hours tinkering with and analyzing my own Timeline, and since putting it into practice, I've found that not only does this principle convert more of the casual new visitors into Followers, but also encourages interaction and sharing from the community.

Below, an example of a balanced Timeline--this looks at the "ideal" composition of your Last 10 Tweets (most recent to oldest):

ABOVE THE FOLD (Recall, on mobile, "above the fold" refers to the First Four Tweets visible on someone's Timeline on mobile, before Twitter inserts the 'Who to Follow' box. As 80% of Twitter's traffic comes from mobile, the quality of your First Four Tweets plays a critical role in converting non-Followers into Followers.):

1. Your Tweet: Share something personal, an observation—a photo you took, often works great. This could be something related to your work, as long as you don't make it too dry and academic. [Make sure you Like any responses to your Tweet].

2. Reply to someone who responded to an earlier Tweet from earlier in the day or a Tweet from a day or so ago. This refreshes the Tweet--when people see your Reply, some may review the original Tweet and Retweet it, if they missed it earlier. More on this in the Strategic Reply chapter.

3. Retweet and Like something interesting from one of your Followers with a low Follower count. Choose someone who has Retweeted you in the past, and if this Tweet gets a lot of Retweets, they may gain some Followers and, return the favor by Retweeting you more often. [Note: Read the cautions about

Retweeting in the Strategic Retweet Section].

4. Your Tweet: Make it something interesting and fun—could be a trivia/stat related to your industry, or your unique POV on a Trending Topic, which allows you to take advantage of the Trending hashtag; use a visual.

   [Note: Strive to maintain at least one Retweet or Reply in your First 4 "above the fold" Tweets. This is a good signal to potential new Followers that you are not a Bot.]

   BELOW THE FOLD:

5. Your Tweet: Make this not related to work. Excluding an image is fine (so you're not overloading your Timeline with too many images). Skip inserting a link, if that doesn't reduce the impact of the Tweet.

6. Retweet someone's entertaining Reply to your Tweet: Encourages people to Reply more thoughtfully to your Tweets when they know that you Retweet the best Replies.

7. Your Tweet: Join a conversation and share your perspective or simply state something positive. Include an annotated visual. Use your judgment on whether linking out vs. skipping the link would be better.

8. Retweet someone with a high Follower count—use this strategically, as outlined in the Strategic Retweet section.

9. Your Tweet: Share an original thought, perhaps on a Trending Topic, so you can take advantage of the trending hashtag.

10. Your Tweet: Share an original thought.

Note: The exact order and formulation described above is less important. The more important thing to remember is to not let too many of your own Tweets clump together in your Timeline, especially in the First Four Tweets. A 60-40 ratio (your Tweets vs. Retweets) is also fine, but remember that every Tweet on your Timeline, whether yours, or something you Retweeted, should be a quality Tweet, and serve a very specific purpose, from helping get one of your Followers more exposure, to surfacing an older Tweet.

Now, this rule of not getting too chatty is probably bad news for those of you who love Twitter chats and live Tweet conferences. Until Twitter rolls out a better chat room system, my suggestion is to limit how chatty you get on Twitter—1-2 Tweets per Twitter chat and conference should suffice. When joining chats, try to reply to 2-3 people on the chat with your POV, as that increases the likelihood of your Tweet getting Liked/Retweeted by multiple people.

In general, Tweet less, and promote your content more, using the Strategic (Reply, Retweet, Like, DM) and other tactics outlined in this book.

Anatomy of a Winning Tweet

Earlier I noted that you get about ten seconds to impress someone who lands on your Twitter profile into Following you. But you get even less time than that—around five seconds—to catch the attention of someone who happens to be scrolling through their Twitter Newsfeed, and comes across your Tweet. To recap, people will see your Tweet in their Newsfeed if they are Following you, or if your Tweet gets Retweeted or Quoted by someone they are Following.

Five seconds is all you have to get them to pause scrolling, focus on your Tweet, and engage with it—(i.e., Retweet, Quote, Reply, Like). So what does the winning Tweet--one that will get Retweeted or Quoted--look like?

1. No:

    a. Shortened words: "gr8" for "great"; "ctr" for "center"; "&" for "and". If you find yourself needing to shorten certain words, look for a better way to rephrase your message.

    b. Tricky spacing: Omitting a space after the period or including too many spaces can also hinder some picky people from sharing it.

    c. Grammatical and factual errors: If these are called out in the comments, it hurts the Tweet's chances of getting Retweets.

    d. Typos: Double check spelling—nothing worse than a mistake getting lots of Retweets.

    e. "-->" and "<--": Inserting arrows in a Tweet, either before quoting a Tweet, or anywhere in the message, is amateurish; avoid.

        Must read --> @handle2 blah blah blah blah

        Or, worse:

        blah blah blah blah @handle2 <-- This!

f. Clich s and generic phrases: "Great article", "good read", "super excited", "amazing" (to describe a food item), "packed room" (to describe an event) are so widely used, that if you want to get Retweeted, find better synonyms.

g. Manual RT: I don't Retweet Manual RTs, and neither should you. Just Retweet, and give the original poster full exposure and credit.

h. Modified Tweet or MT: This is old school, and no reason to use it. Just Retweet.

2. Timing + angle: Come up with an unusual perspective or hit a nerve, especially when tweeting about a trending topic. Before you tweet, run a search (on Twitter, use Advanced Search options if necessary to filter) to see how others have tweeted about what you are looking to also tweet. Look for any phrasing that stirs you in those Tweets–the comments/replies section also offers valuable insights and talking points that you can utilize to refine your tweet. For example, I have often seen replies to a viral tweet provide missing context or corrections, which you can incorporate into yours, thus giving it more punch and relevance. In short, do a quick but thorough analysis on why other tweets on the same topic did well—seek clues in the length, timing, pacing, tone, and style. And if you have a particular turn of phrase that you want to employ, run a search to see if anyone else has used that exact phrase in the same context, and if so, best to avoid duplicating it. Find a better way to say what you want to say, remembering that irony and humor can be reliably good ingredients.

It is helpful to build a list of phrases that you can quickly refer to—include these phrases in your Tweet if applicable. Some of my best Tweets took hours to craft. And people can tell when you've put in the effort.

If posting an article, don't simply parrot the headline in the message of your Tweet. Put your own, better spin on it.

If you're forced to Tweet about mundane business articles ("7 Relationship Building Tips", "10 Business Networking Apps Every Entrepreneur Needs" etc.), find one great point from the article, and highlight that, using guidance in 3, 4, and 9 below.

3. Length: 80-100 characters long. Shorter Tweets win because everyone appreciates artful brevity. Twitter limits you to 140-characters per Tweet, and some people get around this by splitting their thoughts into multiple numbered Tweets (1/, 2/, 3/, and so on—the so-called Tweetstorm). My preferred approach, If you need to pack in more information into a Tweet:

    a. Create a narrative for your Tweet—it could be up to 280 characters long. Overlay this narrative onto a relevant image, using AfterPhoto, PowerPoint or Word, and save it to your camera roll. Next, compose a Tweet with a short—80-100 characters—description, upload your new image-with-narrative, and Tweet that. This way, you're more than doubling the usual characters allowed per Tweet, while also using a relevant, memorable visual—this becomes an artisanal Tweet that few will dare to steal.

    b. If you need to use text only, use the "Notes" app on iOS (you can also use Notepad, PowerPoint, Word) to compose what you need to say, take a screen shot of that, and upload with the Tweet.

    c. Save people a click: Sometimes it works best to share a screenshot of the most gripping/relevant passage of an article that you wish to share, instead of including a link to it, in your Tweet. So take the screenshot, crop it using your Like photo app, save it to your camera roll, and—this can really make a difference—annotate using an app like Skitch. Underlining or circling certain words or sentences can help focus the reader's eyes immediately, especially if it is a fairly big block of text. Always preview what the image looks like in Tweet Draft mode, and ask yourself—if I saw this in my feed, would I expand the Tweet and review the attached image.

4. Visuals: Include a great, relevant visual (animated GIF, JPG/PNG, video, Vine) in 60% of your Tweets: Use Twitter like Instagram, minus the annoying multiple hashtags.

    a. Tweets with visuals take up more space in a Timeline, so they tend to stick out in a sea of Tweets that don't contain a visual. Important: Do NOT use random image just for the sake of including an image—and stay away from busy, overly styled infographics—these turn me off, personally.

    b.   Make images stand out more by annotating and enhancing (sharpening, reducing shadows) them. I've had repeated success sourcing images off Twitter, enhancing them, and uploading with a Tweet—and they've received more shares than the Tweet from which I sourced the image. Note: If you know the provenance of the image, always credit the source, and sometimes the best way to do this is to mark the image with a small "Source: ___"

    c.   Let the image do the talking—best not to over explain it.

    d.   Don't overdo it with images: Sometimes, people just want to hear you say something intelligent, sans a visual. And don't go overboard with annotating every visual you use.

5. Aesthetics: The appearance of a Tweet—how it looks--can determine whether or not it gets any love, especially when replying to tweets.

For example, a Tweet that looks like the one below (if you are still on versions of the Twitter app that allow you to customize your reply to post your content before the handles, turning it into a "Mention"):

> This is what I have to say @handle1 @handle2 @handle3 @handle4

Will get more attention and Retweets over one that looks like:

> @handle1 @handle2 @handle3 @handle4 This is what I have to say

A couple of years ago, I started experimenting with restructuring my Replies so that my message went before people's handles, mostly because I personally found it annoying to read Replies that began with a bunch of Twitter handles.

After making this change, I immediately started to notice an uptick in engagement (increase in Likes and Retweets) on

Replies, likely because:

- The Tweet was more pleasing to the eye and the people who came across it were able to focus on my message instead of getting distracted by the handles to which I was replying.

- It exposed the Tweet to more people than just mutual Followers--if you start a reply with the @handle, only overlapping Followers see it.

- People generally assume that the Tweet is not a Reply, but a Mention, especially if it is phrased like a sound bite, and that drives more people to share/Retweet and invites Replies.

Make this one of your key Twitter practices--If your Tweet is a Reply or a Mention always insert your message before their Twitter handle. This will increase your chance of getting Retweeted.

So if their handles are @johnsmith and @noreen_tech your Reply should look like:

Weirdly, top three cities most interested in the Apple Watch are in Australia, according to Google Search Trends! @johnsmith @noreen_tech

NOT

@johnsmith @noreen_tech Weirdly, top three cities most interested in the Apple Watch are in Australia, according to Google Search Trends!

For Mentions, too, instead of putting a "." before the handle to increase exposure, insert your message before the handle.

.@charmin, I love your products! [Avoid]

I love your products, @charmin [Use]

6. A Quoted Tweet can also be a turn off...and seeing too many of these on someone's Timeline implies they can't resist injecting their opinion into every Tweet, so a Quoted Tweet, unless really

well done, can result in little engagement. My rule: Unless you're adding something of value that enhances the Tweet you are quoting, just Retweet—it's nice to give others full exposure on your Timeline.

    a.   No one uses MT for Modified Tweet anymore, so don't feel the need to do this—simply Retweet if you want to share someone's Tweet.

7. Don't repeat phrases, words or emojis you've used in the previous Tweet, unless there is a very good reason to do so.

8. Optimize the content for Twitter's search engine: Journalists, especially, search on Twitter when they want to report on interesting reactions or takes, particularly to breaking news stories, sporting events, award ceremonies, and more. Using phrases like "video" and "photo," if including a photo in your Tweet, can be helpful to get your Tweet in front of people who are searching specifically for photos.

   If you're Tweeting about an incident that occurred to you, use the phrases "I", "my", "me"--your Tweet will be more easily discovered by reporters who are searching for a personal statement.

9. Use links and hashtags sparingly, strategically: Twitter is not Instagram, so don't use too many hashtags. Limit to one hashtag, if you must use hashtags.

   Note: In search results and elsewhere, Twitter now surfaces your Tweet if it contains the same words/phrases that match a hashtag, so it is no longer necessary to hashtag words in Twitter. For example, Twitter treats #digitalmarketing the same as 'digital marketing'—so go ahead and just use the latter. It appears cleaner to the reader. It's fine, however, to use a hashtag when it is specifically branded for a campaign or a product, and in the case of a trending event.

10. Attitude: Skipping punctuation (period, comma) or going all lower case can sometimes boost the impact of a Tweet.

   Do NOT:

a. Cross-post from Instagram, Facebook, or Wordpress.

b. Repeat posts—there's a better way to bump up an older post, as I'll discuss shortly.

c. Autopost and schedule posts: Twitter is live and conversational—if you Tweet and are not able to respond (Like, Reply, Retweet) in a timely manner, people will figure out you are auto posting and stop engaging with you.

d. Have an excessive number of automated Tweets from Fitbit, Runkeeper, Meerkat, Periscope, Swarm/FourSquare, or any other tools that you use to manage Twitter. Delete most automated Tweets from your Timeline, unless there is a strategic reason to display one or two of these, for example, as a humblebrag--if you attended a particularly great event that you live streamed on Meerkat or Persicope, or if you ran 38 miles and want fellow athletes to know that.

Some of my Tweets that did well

Here are some of my tweets that did well because they hit a nerve, offered a unique point of view, or weren't afraid to discuss topics many shy from discussing. Visit @hackthebird on Twitter for more examples.

 @Khanoisseur

Every tech conference

1:32 PM - 18 Jan 2015

2,105 Retweets 2,458 Likes

Hit a nerve

Adam Khan
@Khanoisseur

Electric cars, charging stations in garages 1907-1912

5:36 PM - 15 Feb 2015

481 Retweets 580 Likes

Always aim to present a unique angle in your tweets. Historical facts do well—my series of tweets on early 1900s electric cars collectively got over 2000 Retweets.

Adam Khan @Khanoisseur · 6 May 2015
2015 is everything they said it would be.

> En route, in Uber. Instacarted some wine to your place. See you in 10.

> Perfect, Seamless on its way, and Netflix all queued up.

🗨 24   ↻ 353   ♡ 413

Adam Khan @Khanoisseur · 8 Jul 2015
Garrulous 8 yo niece with the crucial question

> Excited to visit?

> Yes

> You'll love it--plenty of parks and playgrounds and hiking trails. Lots of museums too!

> Is your wifi fast

🗨 36   ↻ 986   ♡ 1.3K

(See @HacktheBird for more examples of "viral tweets")

Tweet timing and frequency

What is the best time to Tweet, so you can get Retweeted more?

This is a question I get a lot in my Twitter boot camps. Short answer: If you get really good at Twitter, if you are putting out great content, being generous and sharing content from others (Following the 70-30 Rule), people will turn on notifications for your Tweets, so they don't miss a single Tweet. Once you reach this point, it is somewhat irrelevant when you Tweet, because your most ardent fans will get alerted when you have tweeted and help you boost the signal.

However, balance is also important here...if you're blowing up people's notifications all the time with junk Tweets, they'll mute you, and some may even un-Follow you. Know your content production limits, and read your audience. Tweet with enough frequency to keep people returning to your Timeline, to check out Tweets they may have missed, and use your judgment on how chatty you should get.

I tend to average 8-12 Tweets per day (including Replies and Retweets), spreading these out over the course of 12 hours, so it doesn't annoy people too much, and allows what I've Tweeted to soak up some impressions, Retweets and Likes. This is an important point— any time you Tweet/Retweet something, you want it to be meaningful, and allow people the opportunity to see what you've Tweeted, before distracting them with another Tweet. People are more likely to turn on Notifications for your Tweets if you're not too chatty and produce quality content that you spread out over the course of a few hours.

When you Retweet one of your top Followers and Retweeters, it is especially important to show them that your Retweet is helping them get additional Retweets and Followers, so best to not let their Tweet disappear off the "First Four Tweets" on your Timeline, and defeat the purpose of Retweeting them.

Getting to the first 100,000 Followers

1. Fix your Bio, Profile and Header pictures (refer to the Bio chapter for guidance).

2. Groom your Timeline according to the 70-30 Rule, paying particular attention to deleting excessive number of the Following kinds of Tweets:

   - General complaining and snark about airlines, restaurants, coworkers
   - Questionable Tweets/Retweets: Lewd, racist, sexist jokes).
   - Bot and automated Tweets: Horoscopes, Runkeeper, Fitbit, Nike, Meerkat, Periscope, Follower/Un-Follower summary, "I liked a YouTube vide" etc.).
   - Tweets about music awards, sports, and politics.
   - Too many consecutive replies and comments.

   (Note, if you must Tweet to get a customer service issue resolved, delete the Tweets once that issue is addressed…or once the conversation has switched to DM…no reason to let those Tweets hang out on your Timeline. It's annoying and rude to subject your Followers to a dozen Tweets about your airline fiasco, and can hurt your chances of getting Followed).

3. Make sure your First Four Tweets, "above-the-fold" Tweets-- i.e. the four Tweets people see on mobile (remember, 80% of Twitter's traffic comes on mobile) before Twitter inserts the "Who to Follow" box--present you in the best light. Include at least one quality Retweet and one terrific Reply in your First Four. And make your most popular Tweet your pinned Tweet (which will only be seen on Desktop).

4. Get everyone that likes you in real life and connections from other social networks to Follow you on Twitter. Email or let current and past coworkers, friends, acquaintances from your place of worship, gym, yoga class, volunteer orgs, current and former lovers…you get the idea. Periodically post links to your best Tweets on Facebook and LinkedIn.

5. When you attend events and they ask you to create a name badge, always write your Twitter handle down, along with your name, and ask people to Follow you. Some will probably say they're not very active on Twitter—that's okay—Follow them any way.

6. Include your Twitter handle in your email signature, on business cards, and in bios on other social networks—this is usually a good signal to others that you are willing to engage with them on Twitter.

7. Follow lots of people that pass the Timeline Test, especially interesting people with under a thousand Followers. This may seem counterintuitive, however, people with a small but engaged following are likely to be more enthusiastic Retweeters and Mentioners than bigger accounts. Some of your best Retweets will be a result of someone with a small following Retweeting you, and catching the attention of an Influencer with a massive number of Followers.

8. When you follow lots of people, add them to segmented Lists so you can easily engage with them by Liking or Retweeting them. Create segmented Private Lists of Targets--people that you want to Follow you back—and add your Targets to these Lists (see the chapter on Lists for more).

   For example, create a Private List called "Target Journos NYC" for all the journalists in NYC that you want to Follow you back. Create similar Private Target Lists for other kinds of Followers you're looking to target, including local businesses (restaurants, supermarkets, salons, coffee shops, music venues…), brands, policy makers, and more. Engage them in conversations and RT and Like their Tweets, Following the 70-30 Rule.

9. Create a Retweet circle: These are people who will Retweet you and that you Retweet in exchange. It could be a group of no more than 15 people, but add them to a Private List…call it Retweet Circle or something meaningful, and turn on notifications for them, so you get alerted when they Tweet and you can be the first one to Retweet.

10. Retweet the best content from your Retweet Circle using the 70-30 Rule, and encourage them to Retweet you back.

11. Use the guidance in the <u>Get Strategic with Likes (1-100 Rule)</u> chapter to continually grow and engage your audience.

12. Take a break: It's easy to get burnt out on Twitter. But don't give up. <u>Take a "break"</u>.

Use Lists to Target Content, Gain and Engage Followers

Using Twitter's Lists strategically helped me in ways that I couldn't have imagined when I first heard about this feature. Lists are now my go-to, and they are going to become your best friends, too. Effective use of Lists will not only improve your overall Twitter experience, but they will also help you gain and keep Followers, find an audience for your content quickly, and get your Tweets in front of them. I've created over 150 Lists (both Public and Private), and it's a crucial tool in staying on top of what the 8000+ people that I Follow are Tweeting.

Why are Lists so important? Unlike Facebook, where an algorithm is constantly figuring out what kind of content (babies, engagements, weddings, entertainment, sports, humor, politics) you like and puts that content in your Newsfeed (yes, you only see a fraction of all content your Friends are posting, because of this algorithm), Twitter displays all Tweets from the people you are Following in your Newsfeed. Depending on how many people you Follow, your Newsfeed could become overwhelming. Twitter's Lists will help you channel this "fire hose" of content into more manageable streams, and once you start using these, you'll truly get hooked on Twitter.

Quick primer: Twitter lets you create two kinds of Lists:

Public: Anyone can see the name and Members of this list, and when you add accounts to a Public list, they will be notified. This can be used strategically, as I will outline in a bit, to get people to Follow you back. An account can be added to multiple Public lists, which can also be very helpful, as I'll show you in a second.

Private: Only you can see the name and Members of this list, and when you add accounts to a Private list, they will NOT be notified. There are reasons why you should use Private lists, and I will outline those too. An account can be added to multiple Private lists also.

The key thing about Lists is that they help you segment Twitter accounts that are of interest to you by profession (Journalists, Policymakers, Artists, Businesses), Geography (New York City, San Francisco, Copenhagen), and even by the type of content your Followers seem to like (themes).

When you add people to Lists, you can Follow their Tweets indirectly—i.e., without actually Following them directly/natively, by clicking on the Follow button on their Twitter profile.

Their Tweets, however, will not display in your Home Timeline. You will have to go to each individual List you created in order to read their Tweets.

But as I will show you in the Strategic Add-to-List chapter, adding people to Lists will help you gain and retain Followers.

So let's get started with creating Lists (if you're not familiar with List creation, some tips here: https://support.twitter.com/articles/76460-using-twitter-lists)

You're going to create the Following Lists—type noted in "()":

1. 'Like People' (Private): Add to this list friends, co-workers, those you've met on Twitter who have become your best Followers because they actively Like and Retweet you. Add up to 100 people here, and if you need to add more people, create a second Private List called 'Like People 2' and so on—it's more manageable this way. Every day you'll spend a few minutes looking at the Tweets on this List and Like and Retweet (based on 70-30 Rule). It's a good way to stay on top of the Tweets from your most loyal Followers.

2. 'Target' (Private): These are people that you want to Follow you back. I'll let you decide who your targets should be, but my Target List includes journalists, VCs, artists, policy makers, CEOs, bloggers, restaurants, chefs and others. You can create multiple numbered Target Lists, if you're targeting more than a 100 people. I'll show you how you can convert Targets into Followers. Today, my Target lists have 300 new people, and I have converted 90% of the people on my original Target list into Followers.

3. 'Top Followers' (Private): Once someone influential from your 'Target' List—say, a journalist with thousands of Followers, starts Following you, you will move them from the 'Target' to the 'Top Followers' List—this becomes one of the Lists you visit frequently, to review the Tweets from your 'Top Followers' List, and interact with them in a way that rewards their decision to Follow you. Note: While The 'Top Followers' List will contain

your most influential Followers, there's no reason why you cannot also add them to both the 'Like People' Lists.

4. 'Local Love' (Public): To this List you will add local businesses, including restaurants, galleries, coffee shops, government agencies, malls, etc. You can call this list anything you desire, and can probably come up with something more creative. You want this list to be public because you want these businesses to receive a notification, which could potentially result in them Following you.

5. 'New Following' (Private): This is where you'll add the people you recently started Following—cap this off at a 100 people to start with, and then each time you add a new member, remove an older member. I'll explain how you'll use this List in a few.

6. Audience Targeting Lists (Private): Add people to Private Lists based on the type of content they previously indicated an interest in (Liked/Retweeted/Replied to both your Tweets and others' Tweets): I've found it helpful to maintain lists of people that have previously shared or responded well to specific kinds of Tweets. For example, if someone has Retweeted or Replied to a Tweet about Startups, I'd add them to a List called 'Aud Startups'—'Aud' being short for "audience". My Audience Lists Tweets tend to mirror the themes I Tweet about, but I also add people who liked Tweets from subject matter experts to this list, so I can easily target them when I post something that might be of interest to them. For example:
    a. 'Aud NYC Photos': People who like photos of NYC
    b. 'Aud Startups': People who like news/metrics about startups
    c. 'Aud Tech': People who like general tech news
    d. 'Aud History': People into historical facts
    e. 'Aud Science': People who like science-related Tweets
    f. 'Aud UX': People into good UX practices

7. 'Retweeted Me' (Private): These are people who have recently Retweeted you. Add them to this list so you remember to return the favor.

8. Lists for People by Geography: You'll grow faster on Twitter if you have a diverse Following, especially when you have people who live outside your own state or country sharing your content. I create Private and Public lists ('New York City', 'San Francisco', 'Copenhagen' etc.), based on where interesting

people that I want to Follow (directly and indirectly) are located, and add people to these lists. It makes it easier to reach out to people in specific cities when I can quickly look them up in my Twitter Lists.

9. 'Journalists' (Public): You'll add journalists that you want to Follow to this List, and you can refine the segment further, and name these Lists as best suits you. For example, I have the Following Lists, where I've added Journalists by type (and they may share Members, because a journalist in the 'NYC Journos' List could also be in 'Tech Journos' List if they happen to cover Technology):
   a. 'Tech Journos'
   b. 'NYC Journos'
   c. 'DC Journos'

Get Strategic with Likes: 1-100 Rule

The Like has become the single most used Twitter feature for me. Believe it or not, early in my Twitter evolution, that Like button helped me attract—and, just as important, keep--more Followers than my Tweets.

As you probably know, the Like can be used in multiple ways:

1. Bookmark: Liking a Tweet adds it to your Likes tab and you can use this to go back and reference a Tweet later. (I don't use the Like to bookmark, however.)

2. 'Read' notice: Liking a Tweet is also an acknowledgement that you have seen the Tweet.

3. Like: Liking a Tweet could also be considered a high five—you approve of the Tweet.

One of the most important functions of the Like? This:

4. Digital Poke: The Like says, "Come check out my Twitter Timeline." Liking a Tweet is an incredibly powerful way to get people—both your Followers and those who don't yet Follow you—to notice you and visit your Timeline. [People would have to enable Notifications for Likes to see that you have Liked their Tweets.]

As we'll soon see, you can strategically wield the Like to gain specific kinds of Followers.

I Like Tweets a lot, mostly to let people know that I saw and liked their Tweet. I do this because I've often had people tell me that the reason they don't Tweet is because they don't think anyone is listening to them—that Tweeting feels like talking to an empty room.

I particularly like to Like the Tweets of people who are starting out on Twitter or have less than a thousand Followers. I was there once, and I remember how great it felt to have someone with lots of Followers Like one of your Tweets.

At the time of this writing, I have 260,000+ Likes. Compare that to the # of Tweets I posted—5500—that's a Tweet to Like ratio of roughly 1:50. My goal is to Like 100 Tweets for every Tweet I post.

Note: There are now tools available that let you automate your Likes, based on key words ("startup", "growth hacking" "social media" etc.) contained in Tweets. I know several people that use such tools, and it's a bit comical to see the same accounts Like Tweets that contain such keywords almost as soon as the Tweet is posted. Do not use automated tools to Like, not only can this result in you accidentally Liking an obscene Tweet, but also because once people realize you are using such a tool, they will likely stop engaging with you.

Liking Tweets is also a great way to retain Followers—Liking someone's Tweet lets them know you have seen it, that's a wonderful way to show someone you are engaged and listening.

One of the key benefits of getting people to Like you back: The action will show up in the #Discover/Activity screen (Note: At the time of writing, Twitter had removed this screen, but I'm betting they will bring back an improved version). Similar to the Facebook ticker, this screen shows you what people you are Liking and Retweeting, in real-time. In other words, just like the Facebook "Like" the act of someone Liking a Tweet will, technically, expose your Tweet to others who may not be Following you!

So the more you condition others to Like Tweets, the better because this is free exposure for you in the Activity screen. Twitter has also experimented with showing Tweets that have been Liked by people you Follow in the main Timeline and in the Magic Recs DMs—the latter is a message that alerts you when certain Tweets are getting a lot of Retweets or Likes from people you know.

In summary, there are four great reasons to Like people's Tweets:

1. If you Like the Tweets of the people that don't Follow you, they will visit your Timeline, and if you observe the 70-30 Rule, you stand a good chance of being Followed.

2. People will likely Like your Tweets in return—your Tweets look good when they accumulate Likes—and the more Likes a Tweet gets, the more likely that a new person landing on your Twitter is to Follow you.

3. When someone Likes your Tweets, you will get exposure via the Activity screen, and maybe even in the main Timeline and Magic Recs DM.

4. People like it when you Like a Tweet—it lets them know that you saw their Tweet. It reminds them that you exist. And if they haven't hopped on to your Twitter recently, Liking one of their Tweets draws them back into your Timeline to see the last few Tweets, and that could result in more Retweets and Likes.

Before we get into the many ways in which you can use the Like to grow your Followers, some rules:

First rule of the Like Club: DO NOT LIKE YOUR OWN TWEET! Sorry about the caps, but it looks really weird when people do that. Thankfully, if you get really good with the tips below, you won't ever need to pity Like your own Tweets.

Second Rule of the Like Club: Do not Like bot Tweets (more on this below).

Third Rule of the Like Club: Put some heart into it. Take some time to read the content of a Tweet before you Like it. You don't want to Like something offensive and have that show up in your Likes history, for your other Followers to see.

With that, some powerful ways in which you can wield the Like to get new Followers and engage with existing ones:

1. Search for and Like Tweets related to your last few Tweets. Say your last Tweet was about the Apple Watch. Search for Apple Watch, then:

   a. Click on 'More from people you Follow" and Like the relevant Tweets. Like Notifications, if turned on, will bring these people back to your Timeline and if they see the relevant Apple Watch Tweet, they might Like or Retweet it. Some may decide to Follow you back.

   b. Go back to Previous Screen (the Search Results page). Click on the All Tweets tab. This will display all Tweets containing "Apple Watch." Now before you start Liking Tweets here, do yourself a favor and weed out the bot Tweets—quickly scroll down and see if you can spot a pattern in the Tweets. Are dozens of them saying the same thing, for example, "Only 53 Apple stores Will Carry The Apple Watch"? If so, these are from bots. Are there any other patterns? Make a mental note of those too. Sometimes it helps to refine your search further using phrases that only humans would use—for example, "can't wait," as in "can't wait to get the Apple Watch." Start Liking the Tweets that you think are interesting and which do not fall into a pattern.

2. Like Tweets from Like People, Top People and Target People Lists (at a minimum, you want to engage with these people at least once a day, by Liking their Tweets. You may have created other Lists, and you may want to review and Like the Tweets from those Lists as well.

    a. "Deep Fave": Don't just Like (Fave) one Tweet on someone's Timeline, Fave 5-6 Tweets from the same person, including any Tweets where they're Replying to others. You'll condition them to do the same, while creating the possibility that some of the people they're Replying to—and some of these may not be Following you or even know that you exist, will come to your Profile as a result of the Like, and decide to Retweet, Like or Follow you.

3. Like the Tweets of people who have Liked the Tweets of people from your Like People, Target People, and Top People list—especially those who don't already Follow you: Say you Follow Jack, and Jack is in your Like People's List. Look at who has Liked Jack's last few Tweets, and then hop over to their Twitter Profiles and Like a few of their Tweets.

4. Retweet someone and then look at their:

    a. Last few Tweets on their Timeline: Like those Tweets, especially any Retweets and Replies containing two or more people. Notifications will do their magic here too—i.e. some will come back and visit you, and may decide to Follow you, since you've Retweeted someone familiar to them.

    b. Likes (click on the Likes tab in their profile)—then Like the Tweets they have Liked. When people hop over to your profile to check you out, they'll see you have Liked one of their friends or recent Twitter interactions, and likely Follow you, or at least remember you.

c. List of Followers: Like the Tweets of people that are Following the person you just Retweeted. When I last ran this test, I got over a hundred people to Follow me, simply by Liking their Tweets (and I Followed back several of the ones that did Follow me).

d. Monitor who all is Retweeting your Retweet—some of these Retweets may be coming from people who do not Follow you: Hop over to their Timeline and Like a few of their Tweets. Follow them if they happen to be interesting and/or add them to a Public List, so they get additional notifications.

5. Like a Reply someone posted to your most recent Tweet, instead of replying immediately. This lets them know that you have seen their comment. Then, if their Reply is exceptional, Retweet it in a few hours (helps you satisfy the 70-30 Rule). This refreshes/bumps the conversation, and a new set of people who previously had not seen original Tweet will now be exposed to it, because they saw your Reply.

a. Note: You may also send them a Direct Message to say something nice, like how much you enjoy their Tweets. This is always good gesture, when you need to delay responding to someone.

b. Deep Fave people who respond to your comments. This conditions them to do the same.

c. Sometimes, a Reply to your Tweet may not be the most ideal to Like because they said something weird or offensive—it happens. In such cases, best not to Like the Reply, but wait a few minutes and Like some of their other non-weird Tweets. If they're smart, they'll get the hint that you don't encourage weird comments in the future.

d. Delaying the Like to their Reply selectively, after you've posted a couple of new Tweets, will expose those new Tweets to them, if they come back to your Timeline as a result of the Like.

6. Search for and Like the Tweets pertaining to Meetups, conferences, and Twitter chats related to your profession and

interests, plus Tweets from people about your Like sporting events and TV shows. [See the chapter on Chats.]

Temporarily modify your bio prior to Liking such Tweets. For example, if Liking Tweets about a game in which your Like team is playing, indicate you are a fan of that team in your bio. You may have to take something out of your bio to make the space, but this is temporary. Once the game is over, and you've gained a few Followers as a result of Liking their Tweets, you can return to your default bio. Follow some of these people back if you need to, but more importantly, remember to add these new Followers to a Public List, so the next time you are Tweeting about that team, you can ping them by Liking their Tweets.

When Liking Tweets from conference goers, you'll usually get better results in terms of converting them into Followers if you Like the Tweets closer to the Lunch break, when they have a chance to catch up with Notifications.

7. If a celebrity has a birthday, Tweet out well wishes, or Retweet someone who is wishing the celebrity Happy Birthday, and then search for and Like the Tweets from others wishing that celebrity "Happy Birthday". Search for Tweets with keywords like ("same day" and "share") for people that have Tweeted that they share a birthday with said celebrity. Note, this is a low-percentage return, but does work.

8. Like Tweets with the #FF hashtag. These typically contain multiple Twitter handles and with one Like, you are potentially sending a notification to multiple people.

9. In general, Like any Tweets that have multiple Twitter handles (people, businesses) tagged, as this allows you to maximize the impact of one Like, by sending notifications to multiple people.

10. Like Tweets of new Followers of someone who just blew up big time on Twitter. Say John had this awesome Tweet that got picked up widely and he now just added 50 new Followers. Hop over to his Followers list and start Liking Tweets of people who started to Follow him. The reason: These people are active on Twitter (if they just Followed him) and if they receive your Like notification, they may decide to Follow you, or they might Like a few of your Tweets.

11. If you've been recently been Followed by a journalist, a Big Account, or anyone Verified, Like the Tweets of their colleagues and peers. When people visit your profile and scan your Followers List, they'll notice that one of their colleagues or peers recently started Following you, and they might decide to Follow you as well, especially if you've recently Retweeted their colleague/peer--make sure this Retweet is clearly visible in the Top 4 Tweets (See the 'Strategic Retweet' Section for more).

12. Look at your Newsfeed. See which Tweets recently got Retweeted and Liked and Comments. Hop on to the profiles of these people who Retweeted, Liked and Replied/Commented, and Like some their Tweets. Add them to Lists, and Follow if necessary. If they have notifications turned on, they will notice.

13. When you Like can be more important than when you Tweet. Liking at odd hours--late at night and early in the morning is particularly effective because it helps you cut through the noise. Some of my best Follows have come from engaging people via the Like at odd hours.

14. Add people who have recently Followed you to a New Followers List (make this a Private List) and Like their Tweets regularly for a few days. This will condition them to your Liking habits and encourage them to Like in return.

15. Be Liking all the time—any time you have a few spare minutes, hope on and Like some Tweets in your Newsfeed. If you discover any new people in your Newsfeed, as a result of Retweets/Replies/Mentions, hop on to their Timeline and Like their Tweets.

16. If people you are Following do not Follow you back and do not respond to your Likes, don't give up Liking. Likely they have turned off notifications turned off for Likes, or don't really use the Likes as a Like, but I've noticed that increasingly people who did not use to Like, have started to do so. In fact, I've had recent success getting the attention of such people through not giving up on Liking.

    Another approach you can use in such cases: Like the Tweets where they are engaged in conversations with 2 or more people. If those people notice your Like and Follow you, you've at least maximized the use of your Like.

Converting your Targets into Followers

Converting people in your (Private) Target Lists into Followers could take anywhere from a few seconds to a few months, so be disciplined and patient.

Maintaining a "groomed Timeline" and obeying the <u>70-30</u> and <u>1-100</u> Rules are the foundation for enabling that conversion.

Here's how I got an influencer with hundreds of thousands of Followers to follow me, but you can apply this process to anyone in your Target List.

1. Groom your Timeline using the 70-30 Rule.

2. Research:

    a. When do they Tweet (time of day) and what do they Tweet about (topics)?

    b. What is their style of Tweeting? Do they Reply frequently and promptly? Do they Retweet others? Do they Like Tweets? (All of these are easy to tell by looking at their Timeline).

    c. Who do they interact with most? Scan their Timeline to spot their closest friends and allies—the ones they interact with/Retweet the most, and add their Friends to a Private List?

    d. Personal background:

        1. Where did they go to school?

        2. What was their first job out of college?

        3. Read latest news and old articles about and by them: Build a fact base. I maintain a fairly elaborate spreadsheet about my Targets.

3. Add them to a memorably named Public List ('VC Savants' for VCs that you are targeting, for example) and Follow them, but

time your add-to-list and Follow for when they are not getting Followed by tens of people (i.e. after they got a big Retweet or a major write up). Let the dust settle, and execute this Step during a slower period, when your Follow is more likely to be noticed (via the "digital pokes" -- alerts on their Notifications screen). If they Follow you at this point, skip to Step 8 below.

4. Set Alerts for when they Tweet and be the first to Retweet one of their good Tweets. When that Tweet takes off (gets lots of Retweets), they'll attribute part of its success to your Retweet. Don't Retweet them too much—maybe once or twice a month. Like their Tweets, though, especially the Tweets that aren't seeing much action. It is easier to stick out when they check the Tweet to see who Liked.

5. Make friends with their friends—Follow their friends and get their friends to Follow you (using this same approach). Set alerts for when their friends Tweet. Like/Retweet their Tweets and their friends' Tweets based on the 70-30 Rule. If they have notifications turned on, they will notice you. They might not Follow you right away, but they are noticing you.

6. Reply or Quote to them and their friends in an intelligent manner (Follow the rules laid out in the Conversations chapter). If your contributions are awesome, their fans will Retweet, Like or Reply, which sends more notifications their way.

7. When the conversion happens—i.e. they start Following you, do not DM them immediately to thank them!

8. Like a few of their Tweets every day.

9. Retweet them once-twice a month.

10. Engage in a conversation or reply to them once or twice a month, but no more than that, and when you do say something, make it count…refer to the chapter about Conversations, for more. If your contribution is valuable, you might get a big Retweet out of it.

How to Find an Audience for Your Tweet

If you are building up your Twitter Following—that is, you don't have hundreds or thousands of engaged Followers yet, you don't have people who have notifications turned on for your Tweets, or are otherwise actively monitoring your account, and are Retweeting everything you put out like crazy, you'll need to work harder to find an audience for whatever it is that you want to say. There are a couple of great ways to do this. Let's take the example of a photo you want to Tweet about, say, New York City. You took this amazing picture and now you want to share it with others.

Here's what you would do to get that Tweet with the photo maximum exposure:

1. Tag the Twitter accounts that you know like to share photos about New York City—for example, @everythingnyc, @nyc and @nycfeelings frequently like to Retweet people that are sharing photos and content about NYC. You can discover such accounts by running a Twitter keyword search for "NYC" and filtering for photos. Note the accounts that are frequently sharing NYC photos, especially those that are Retweeting people. Add these accounts to a Private List (see the chapter on creating Content Targeting Lists) called "Aud NYC Photos"—these are people who you know are receptive to that specific kind of content.

2. You can also tag the Twitter handles of businesses, brands, park services, landmarks and government organizations that you know have offices, stores on the street where you took the picture (you can tag up to 10). Search for these businesses on Twitter and look up their Twitter handle. Try to find businesses that are active on Twitter—look at their Timeline to determine when their last Tweet was (see examples below).

3. Say something polite, humorous or poetic (flattery works, always): "Enjoying an effulgent afternoon in the Lower East Side. NYC, I never want to leave you!!" Throw in an emoji.

4. After you Tweet, quickly run another search for "NYC"—this time, not necessary to filter for Photos--and see who else has been Tweeting about NYC, and Like roughly fifty Tweets that you like. If they have notifications turned on, some of these people will come to your Timeline, see your NYC Tweet, and

some may Like, Retweet or Follow you.

5. When people/businesses Retweet or Like your Tweet, add them to the "Aud NYC Photos" Private List, and retarget them the next time you post similar content, by Liking their Tweets. If some of these people Follow you, it helps to Follow them back, and periodically Retweet them, or Direct Message them to compliment their Tweets.

6. Creating segmented Audience Lists (Private) and adding people that you know like specific kinds of content to these lists is a great way to quickly reach out to people when you have Tweeted something that you know they are going to like and share.

7. Another approach to finding an audience for your thoughts: Join Conversations, as outlined in the next chapter.

Adam Khan
@Khanoisseur

Georgetown sunsets are next level stuff.

6:05 PM - 24 Oct 2014

49 Retweets 83 Likes

Georgetown BID, DC Circulator, Fiola and 6 others

5   49   83

Use Twitter's photo-tagging feature—you can tag up to ten Twitter accounts. This not only makes for a sleeker Tweet--because your message isn't overshadowed by Twitter handles--but it's also an excellent way to get around Twitter's character limits, as ten Twitter handles would likely not fit in a message. Plus, your Tweet will get more shares and comments if Retweeted by multiple accounts tagged.

Use this judiciously, though, because you don't want to annoy people by randomly tagging them in photos.

Save your best material for Conversations

Your message can go a lot further if you deploy it in a conversation, especially as you are in the early stages of building a Twitter audience, when you may not have many people actively keeping an eye out for your Tweets.

Joining Conversations and Replying to Tweets is also the most effective way to get people's attention in certain cases. Unlike Likes and Retweets, which may go unnoticed, especially if people you're Retweeting and Liking have notifications turned off--those who get lots of Retweets/Likes generally turn notifications off for these-- Mentions/Replies are more visible. If your reply is on point, it could get more Retweets than the Tweet to which you are Replying, especially if both the original poster and others who see your Reply, Retweet it.

So if you have something great to say, find a conversation that is taking place around that topic. Run a quick Twitter search to discover who all are discussing that topic, and smartly insert your POV. Note, when you run a keyword search on Twitter, you get two sets of results. The Top Tweets tab (on mobile) displays Tweets from people you know (Followers/Following). The All Tweets tab displays Tweets from everyone, and this also includes spam bots. Best to have conversations with people you know. (See the Strategic Like and Strategic Reply chapters for lots of great tips on how to use the Like to gain more exposure for your Replies and to also refresh/boost older Tweets.)

I save away tons of great facts and stats and trivia to be used when the moment is right, rather than posting these as a standalone Tweet, because once you Follow the right people that share your interests, you'll never be at a loss for the opportunity to participate in conversations around your Like topics.

Replying to people who comment on your Tweets is also important--people want to see that you are not a bot, and the 70-30 Rule encourages you to reply to others, while maintaining a balanced, "groomed" Timeline. The key rule about conversations: Be respectful and add something of value that others would be delighted and proud to share.

Here's how to get the most out of Conversations and Replies:

1. Make the Reply memorable--phrase it as a sound bite, as it improves the likelihood of the Reply getting Retweeted. Use a

visual if it helps, as Tweets that have visuals will take up more space and grab the attention of someone scrolling through the Replies.

2. Reply to 2-4 people, selecting a mix of people you already Follow or who Follow you, people that you would like to Follow you, and their propensity to Reply or Retweet (look at their Timeline—do they Reply and Retweet?)

   a. Related hack if you're jumping into a conversation—a Tweet that got Retweeted by a Big Account that you do not Follow, but which is getting a lot of Retweets and Replies, including possibly by people you Follow/Follow you--Find the Tweet on the Timeline of said Big Account. Hit Reply—this will capture both the Big Account's handle and also add the original poster and people you've interacted with in the past. Then insert your comment. **Always insert your comment in front of the Twitter handles** (refer to the Anatomy of the Winning Tweet chapter). Replying to a Tweet that is going viral exposes you to more than just the people you are copying on the Reply—everyone that expands the original Tweet to look at the Replies will see your Reply, especially if you insert your comment before the handles. This is a great way to get in front of journalists who are tracking viral Tweets and examining the responses.

   b. I'm generally not a fan of copying/bringing in people that are not part of the original discussion into the thread, however, this could work if that person happens to be someone with whom you've built a relationship, will value your invite to join, and can enhance the conversation. If your CC backfires, people can ask to take you off the discussion, and even block you.

3. If your Reply is so good that it is getting Retweeted by everyone you copied, other Big Accounts may pick it up, and this usually results in more Retweets and new Followers!

   a. Note, I've seen instances where both the original poster and the Big Account you copied initially do not Retweet the reply, but as they see the flood of Retweets happening, they too will jump in and Retweet your

Reply. In any event, while some that are copied on your Reply might be annoyed that your Reply is getting so many Retweets and blowing up their Notifications, others might actually be happy that their Twitter Profiles are getting more exposure--and they might get a few new Followers too, because your Reply that mentioned them is getting lots of traction.

4. Contribute something of value—maybe an anecdote or a statistic that is relevant to the conversation.

    a. Related, brazenly hawking your own product or service in a Reply is a good way to get ignored. If you need to promote something, insert a link to it in your bio, or post a Tweet about it on your own Timeline, or make it a Pinned Tweet, before entering the conversation. This way, people will check out your profile when you Reply, and it's a much more subtle, better way of sharing your perspective.

    b. If you must take a contradictory position to whatever is being discussed, be polite. I tend not to jump into conversations just to contradict someone, but sometimes this is necessary, especially if you feel someone is spreading misinformation about you, your product or service.

5. Don't get too chatty: When someone Replies to your Tweet, it's okay to simply Like and let them know you've seen their Reply. If their Reply is a question and you're expected to respond, do so, but jump out after 1-2 replies. Getting dragged into a long Twitter back and forth is not good for your groomed Timeline aesthetic, and violates the 70-30 Rule.

    a. Selectively delay the Reply by a few hours. It helps bump your original Tweet and gets it more exposure. Plus, the pause may allow you to formulate a better response.

    b. Here too, phrase your Reply as a sound bite, inserting your message in front of their Twitter handles, and it might get Retweeted by the person you are responding to, as well as by others.

Dave McClure @davemcclure · Jan 4
something missing @wsj story dropping rate US small biz ownership -- feels like
data is off: wsj.com/articles/endan... pic.twitter.com/P7QOMZEQt7

⤶   ↻ 26   ★ 21   • • •   View photo

Marc Andreessen @pmarca · Jan 4
@davemcclure Chain store revolution, etc. and more recently sharply
suppressed credit for non-tech small business startups.

⤶   ↻ 8   ★ 15   • • •

Adam Khan @Khanoisseur · Jan 4
Impact of **student loan** debt on small business formation:
poseidon01.ssrn.com/delivery.php?l... @pmarca @davemcclure

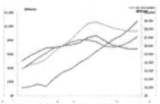

with higher relative growth in student debt show
lower growth in the formation of small
businesses (in this case, firms with one to four
employees).

The correlation makes sense. People normally
have only a certain amount of "debt capacity,"
said Brent W. Ambrose, a professor of risk
management at Pennsylvania State University

business, student loan debt, which cannot be
discharged via bankruptcy, can have lasting
effects later in life and may impact the ability of
future small-business owners to raise capital,"
the study says.

Considering that 60 percent of jobs are created
by small business, "if you shut down the ability

RETWEETS   FAVORITES
118   119

Good example of how a helpful (visuals, well-researched) in a timely
manner (at 4 AM!) resulted in lots of Retweets, thanks in no small
measure to Marc Andreesen (@pmarca and @davemcclure) who
generously Retweeted it.

 **Adam Khan**
@Khanoisseur

Ivanka copied an Italian designer but her lawyer says she's a "high ranking government official" shouldn't have to submit to a deposition

 Bloomberg Politics @ @bpolitics
Ivanka Trump faces courtroom showdown over $785 sandals
bloom.bg/2xUYylH

11:09 PM - 21 Sep 2017

7,279 Retweets **9,753** Likes

Tweeting about politics can be risky for some, but if you make it fact-based, your readers will reward you. This one got over 7000 Retweets.

Adam Khan
@Khanoisseur

Not Photoshop—residential towers in Hong Kong.

If everyone lived at this density, human race would fit in Egypt.

3:41 AM - 15 Mar 2016

Don't Get Too Chatty: Rules for Chats and Live Tweeting Conferences

Twitter Chats

A Twitter chat brings together people to discuss a specific topic. Most chats use a branded hashtag (#MillennialChat, #CSRChat, #SEOTalk). A host posts questions (Tweets marked with Q1, Q2, Q3…) and participants respond with answers (Tweets denoted with A1, A2, A3). Chats typically last an hour. Some important tips when joining chats:

1. Until Twitter rolls out a better chat room system, my suggestion is to limit how chatty you get on Twitter Chats—1-2 Tweets per Twitter chat should suffice. Too many (10 or more) Tweets per chat session will annoy other Followers, and will likely get you Muted or un-Followed.

2. Before you reply, temporarily modify your Bio to signal a strong association with the cause. For example, if you're passionate about CSR and joining a chat about CSR, ensure your bio states that. You may even try temporarily changing your cover picture to something that would resonate with your chat audience.

3. Ensure that your Timeline is groomed according to the 70-30 Rule, and that you don't have any Tweets that run contrary to the sentiment and mission of the chat.

4. Instead of a standalone Tweet with the chat hashtag, reply to 2-3 people on the chat session, with your perspective/POV, as that increases the likelihood of your Tweet getting Liked/Retweeted/Quoted by multiple people. Frame your Reply as a sound bite so it can stand up on its own—increases its chances of getting Retweeted.

5. Insert your Reply before their Twitter handles, as that not only makes for a better looking Tweet, it gets visibility beyond mutual Followers, and both of these factors increase the likelihood of getting a Retweet.

6. Like any Replies to your Tweet to acknowledge that you have seen those. If you need to reply to similar queries, use one

Tweet to do so (copying the people that had similar questions), instead of individual replies.

7. Like as many Chat Tweets that you like as possible, as that gets people to visit your Timeline, gaining exposure for your other Tweets, which could get Shared/Liked. You'll likely gain new Followers if your First Four Tweets are relevant to the chat or are otherwise impressive.

8. Remember the 70-30 Rule about maintaining a diversity of your own Tweets/Retweets when joining chats. This is incredibly critical to converting first time Visitors into Followers.

Live Tweeting Conferences

You can often get more people that are attending a particular conference to Follow you on Twitter by not being physically present at a conference, by Following it on Twitter (dial up the Tweets that reference the conference's unique hashtag) instead. Aside from the $$ and time you'll be saving by skipping the conference, you'll focus better on the conference's Twitter stream when not in a room with spotty Wi-Fi service, surrounded by hundreds of attendees. It always strikes me as a bit weird when you scan a room at a conference to see everyone buried in their phones, actively live tweeting, or trying to keep up with the stream, or juggling work email, or all of the above. Largely the same rules as I outlined for Twitter Chats apply for Live Tweeting conferences: DO NOT LIVE TWEET EVERY THING THAT IS BEING SAID. 1-2 quality Tweets are better than 10 that clog up your Followers' Newsfeeds, which could get you muted or un-Followed. Here are 5 Steps to remotely convert conference goers into Followers:

1. Retweet a good conference-related Tweet (you find these by searching for the conference hashtag: #SXSW, DLD2015, etc.):

    a. When you run a search, Twitter will display people you know (either ones who are Following you or are, Followers) in the Top Search Results. If you see a good Tweet from someone who already Follows you, Retweet them. It's a nice gesture and satisfies the 70-30 Rule. Note: If you're not already Following them, do so and make their day. They may Mention you in a "Thank you for Following me!" Tweet and when their Followers see that, it will drive more eyeballs to your Timeline and handle. If you can't find someone that Follows you to Retweet, Retweet someone that you want to Follow you back. Give them 10 minutes or so to Follow you back.

2. In the meantime, Like around 50 or so conference-related Tweets that you really like, and note down the handles of six people, picking a mix of people with high and low Follower counts, and ones most likely to Retweet or Mention (look at their Timelines). People will usually follow you back or Like some of your Tweets when they notice your Like. Others might mention you and thank you for interacting with them—which raises your visibility among their Followers.

3. Next, take a nice photo of the Speaker or the venue, and tag:

    a. The six people whose handles you've noted down.
    b. The speaker (if you know their handle).
    c. The speaker's employer/company.
    d. The conference organizer.
    e. The person you Retweeted in Step 1 above.
       (Note: If the speaker and their company are not visible on Twitter, go with seven conference attendee handles in 'a' above.)

4. Compose the message of the Tweet: Say something like "Enjoying this conference and learning from so many smart people." Include the conference hashtag.

5. Send the Tweet. The Following things could happen:
    a. Everyone tagged either Retweets or Likes (great looking engagement on that)—with one Tweet you've reached the Followers of everyone who has shared it.
    b. People will Mention/Reply, gaining you additional exposure.
    c. You could get everyone that you tagged who didn't Follow you, to Follow you.
    d. Risk: Some people might get annoyed at being tagged, but on the other hand, if the Tweet does well, and they get indirect exposure as people click through to their Timelines and Follow them, that could be a net positive.

Why this approach works:

    a. Tagging the speaker, their employer/company, and conference organizer, especially, is a safe way to get a Retweet from them, if the photo or comment is particularly flattering or poetic. If the speaker works for a big brand with thousands of engaged Followers, and that brand (if tagged in the photo) Retweets you, you're getting massive exposure, for yourself, and others.

b. Including the person you Retweeted earlier is good insurance against them getting annoyed, while a good signal for others whose Tweets you've Liked, to Follow you, in hopes of a Retweet or a Follow.

c. Others that you tagged in the photo will hop over (if they have notifications turned on) to your Timeline, see that you've Retweeted a fellow conference attendee, and will be motivated to Retweet, Like or otherwise positively respond to your Tweet (the one they were tagged in) in hopes of getting another Retweet.

d. The more Retweets this Tweet gets, the better your chances of getting the people tagged to Follow you, as Retweet or Like notifications become a steady source of reminders about you, especially if the Retweets come over the course of a couple of days.

Live Streaming

Download Periscope and get live-streaming—a far superior approach to live-tweeting. I'd make an exception to my no-hashtag rule and suggest using a relevant hashtag, especially if live tweeting a conference. Otherwise, make sure you use SEO-key words if live tweeting events/topics like breaking news. In your bio, you may also want to let your followers know to turn on notifications for both your tweets and live-streams. One of my most widely watched and retweeted live-streams (Periscopes, as they are called) happened to be about the Russian consulate closing in San Francisco. I heard there was a fire alarm that went off at the consulate earlier and high-tailed it there to live-stream that, only to find the fire had been extinguished. But then, I noticed that the consulate staff were hauling stuff out the front of the building, and decided to live-stream that, which resulted in over a 125,000 viewers.

Adam Khan @Khanoisseur · Sep 1

Stuff being hauled away from **Russian embassy** in San Francisco

ENDED 125.3k Viewers

Adam Khan @Khanoisseur

Stuff being hauled away from Russian embassy in San Francisco — San Francisco, CA, United States

pscp.tv

 597    4.1K   5.2K

Push Notifications: Turn them On

Learning how to use, and cope with, Twitter's Push Notifications on the mobile app—the alerts you get when someone interacts with you on Twitter, helped me grow my Twitter audience quite significantly during the early days. These notifications alerted me in real-time as to who was sharing my Tweets or reacting to them, and it allowed me to quickly reciprocate, either by Liking their tweets or by responding to their comment, and that can go a long way when you're a newbie with a small following. So if you are just starting out on Twitter, and looking to build up your following, turn on your Twitter Push notifications, and the hacks I'm about to outline will make more sense.

Before we get into Push Notifications, remember these notifications are an additional form of notifications that appear as a banner pop up on your phone screen to alert you about an interaction that has taken place regarding your Tweets. These alerts mirror the Notifications that are already going to your Twitter app Notifications Screen. So if you find the Twitter Push Notifications–i.e the banner alerts popping up on your phone–to be overwhelming, turn them off, but make it a habit to check your Twitter Notifications Screen every 30 minutes or so, and review who has been interacting with you. This will help you build a mental map of your most engaged followers, while understanding which tweets are doing well, while providing an opportunity to engage your fans in further conversations.

The Notifications Timeline screen in the mobile app also updates in real-time also, to show you when someone:

(a) Shares your Tweets (as Retweets, Quotes)

(b) Mentions/Replies to your Tweet

(c) Likes (aka Likes) your Tweet

(d) Follows you

More on setting up push notifications here
https://support.twitter.com/articles/20170803-managing-push-notifications-on-twitter-for-iphone

I recommend turning on Twitter push notifications for Mentions/Replies, Retweets, Likes, New Followers, Direct Messages, remembering that if you find all these push notifications are overwhelming you, you can always scale them back to getting notifications just for Mentions and Follows, or whatever makes sense.

Now, some will tell you that turning on Push Notifications for Likes and Retweets can get too noisy and distracting, however, unless you are getting hundreds of Retweets and Likes every day, I'd recommend leaving these on.

Eventually, as you ramp up your Twitter engagement/growth, you may not be able to stay on top of all of the push notifications, and can turn them off, and simply rely on reviewing the Notifications Screen on the app or Twitter website to decide your next course of action, but until you reach that point, keep those push notifications turned on.

The Strategic Follow Back

Following back someone who Follows you should be something you put some careful thought into. There are plenty of people who will Follow you, only to un-Follow you once you Follow them, because they want to maintain a certain ratio of Followers to Following. While you can't prevent this from happening, you can mitigate this by being more selective in who you Follow back.

1. When someone Follows you, don't Follow back immediately. Instead:

    a. Check their Timeline (last 20 Tweets) first to confirm:

        i. They are not a bot: Bots simply Retweet other accounts, and do not produce original content or participate in conversations. Do not Follow bots. If their bio or Tweets indicate they offer a service to buy Followers, that's an instant disqualification. I tend to block such Followers.

        ii. You are not part of a batch Follow: Look at their Following List to see if they are Following thousands of people, and if so, you were likely part of a batch Follow, performed by some tool they are using. Do not Follow back such people. Another clue: See how many people they have Followed since they Followed you—if dozens, they're on a Follower acquisition spree, and you don't want to be a part of that. People who Follow tens of thousands of people generally do not bother to engage with you or share your content.

        iii. Their Tweets are not offensive.

        iv. They Retweet and Reply to others, Following something close to the 70-30 Rule (mix of their Tweets and Retweets, plus Replying).

        v. They offer a unique perspective.

        vi. They are selective in who they Follow—definitely Follow back people who are still feeling their way through Twitter and have low Follower and Following counts, as it encourages them to Tweet more.

b. Once you confirm they are worthy of your Follow, add them to an Audience Type List (Private) so you can ping them when you post content that they might like. For example, if you believe they came to Follow you after Liking your Tweet regarding, say, education policy (easy to tell if you have notifications on for Likes or by glancing at the list of people that have Liked your last Tweet. Conversely, they may have decided to Follow you after you had Liked one of their Tweets regarding education policy, so look at their Timeline for a Tweet that you may have Liked for confirmation—this is the best way to attribute your Liking action to the conversion—i.e., their Follow), or if their bio or Timeline suggests they may have an interest in education policy, add them to a Private List called 'Aud_Ed_Policy' or similar. They'll not receive a notification but now you have identified someone who you can ping when you post another Tweet regarding education policy. You can also add them to a city List, based on where they live.

c. Let a day or two pass, during which time you will likely have posted a few new Tweets that they may have missed. Next:l

   i. Determine if they recently active were on Twitter—i.e., if they Tweeted within the last hour or so—by checking their Timeline, or look at their Likes history, to see if they Liked recent Tweets.

   ii. Like their Tweets that you really like—Like at least 10—I call this the "Deep Fave"—i.e. Liking several Tweets deep in their Timeline.

   iii. Add them to a Public List called 'Education Policy'.

   iv. Follow them. Step "i" above is important because if they tend to get Followed by lots of people, they may not notice your Follow, if they are offline, so for maximum exposure, Follow them when you are reasonably certain they are active, or have been recently active, on Twitter.

This sequence will send several notifications their way (if they have these turned on) and you will be communicating pretty clearly through your actions that you are Following them because of your belief that you share a mutual interest—i.e. education policy. The Deep Fave will tell them that you took the time to read several Tweets, and if you Deep Fave them periodically, you'll condition them to do the same to your Tweets.

Importantly, when you delay Following someone back, they will likely return to your Timeline to refresh their memory about you, and see your new Tweets, which they may have missed, as is pretty common when someone Follows many people.

Because you Deep Faved them, they are likely to return the favor by Liking and even Retweeting a few of your Tweets.

Some may thank you on their Timeline for Twitter love, and when their Followers see this Mention, it may result in more Follows, Likes and Retweets for you.

When you repeat this Follow-back sequence with multiple people, and if it produces additional Likes and Retweets for one of your Tweets, Twitter's Magic Recs may DM mutual Followers to let them know that one of your Tweets is seeing some action, or that you were just Followed by multiple people.

Note: My policy is to Follow people that engage with me frequently— when they Reply, Like and Retweet me, while producing good content, they are certainly worth a Follow. I don't go by how many Followers they have, however.

Never repeatedly Follow and then un-Follow someone. It's annoying, you could get blocked or reported for doing so.

The Strategic Add to List

As I noted earlier, adding people to Lists is a good way to segment your Followers and stay on top of Tweets that you might otherwise miss. When you add someone to a Public List, they get a Notification. When you add them to a Private List, they do not get alerted. In either case, once you add someone to a List, you can read their Tweets without directly Following them. I call this an "indirect Follow".

Some ways in which you can convert people that don't Follow you into Followers by adding them to a Public List:

1. Like a few Tweets and then add someone to a Public List—this signals your interest in them and usually gets their attention, and could potentially result in a Follow, provided:
   a. Your Timeline looks attractive (see 70-30 rule).
   b. They are actively monitoring their Notifications.

2. Add to Public List when you've been rate-limited on Likes: When you cannot Like any more, adding people to Lists is one of two ways in which you can continue to ping people on Twitter, so they come check out your Profile. The other way, sending them a Direct Message, only works if they Follow you, or allow DMs from anyone.

You can also use Lists strategically to convert people that you Follow but that don't Follow you back:

1. If someone (let's call them Target A) you Follow doesn't Follow you back, but you've been Liking and Retweeting them, it's likely that they did not notice your efforts because they did not have Notifications turned on for these. (Check their Likes tab to see if they're actively Liking Tweets—people who actively Like generally also notice when someone Likes them. If they turn out to be actively Liking, but do not respond to your Likes, add them to a Public List. If they still do not respond by Following you back, Retweet one of their peers who happens to follow you (satisfies the 70-30 Rule).

2. If that doesn't result in Target A Following you, un-Follow Target A, and add them to a Public List. Don't get too snarky in naming this list, like calling it "Un-Followed"--be a bit more subtle—a name like "Interesting" would suffice, and pique their interest.

3. Periodically, Like the Tweets from this List. Those who didn't have their notifications turned on previously, may have decided to turn them on, so you may catch their attention with a Like.

Does this approach work? Yes, and I have successfully used this to get people to Follow me. And once they do, I follow them back.

The Strategic Direct Message

The Direct Message (DM) allows you to exchange private messages with a single person or with a group of people. You can send a DM to anyone who Follows you. You can also enable a setting to receive a DM from anyone.

Some key strategic uses of the DM:

1. Like the Like, the DM is a nice little "digital poke": Sending someone a DM is a subtle but effective tactic to get them to visit your Timeline, and see your last few Tweets. Use this to approach to DM people after you've Tweeted about something that you think they are likely to enjoy and share. For example, if one of your Tweets about a particular topic was Retweeted or Commented upon by someone who Follows you, retarget them by sending a DM, AFTER you've posted a new Tweet on the same topic. Simply drop them a line to say something like, "I've been enjoying your Tweets. Hope you are well!" And Like a few of their Tweets prior to the DM for good measure.

2. DM someone that Follows you but who you suspect probably has notifications turned off for Likes and Retweets, AFTER you've Retweeted them, so they recognize your effort, but be chill: The "I've been enjoying your Tweets. Hope you are well!" line is sufficient in this case too.

3. DM Followers a link to your Tweet and ask their opinion. This is usually less noisy than @mentioning them.

4. Do NOT DM someone:

    a. Immediately after they Follow you. It's creepy/rude, and you'll likely be un-Followed.

    b. And ask to Follow you on LinkedIn or other social networks.

    c. A link to the Tweet and ask them to Retweet—while some will agree to RT, it's not fair to put them in a position where they had no choice. Instead, position the Tweet that you want Retweeted at the top of your Timeline (ensure that the Tweet makes it clear that you'd appreciate a RT), and then Follow the advice in 1 above. If they visit your Timeline as a result of your DM, they will notice the Tweet that you want to be Retweeted, and then it's up to them to share that with others.

The Strategic Retweet

Let's recap a couple of points about the Retweet: Beyond the basic act of sharing someone's Tweet, Retweeting is the best way to reward and thank them for Following and interacting with you. Nothing like a good old Retweet to spread some love.

Second, let's review the 70-30 Rule regarding Retweeting: Out of 10 Tweets on your Timeline, 3 should be Retweets. The rationale: When new people come to your Timeline and see you are actively Retweeting others, they are likely to Follow you and Retweet you as well. However, don't overdo the Retweet, otherwise you might be mistaken for a bot, or come off as someone who struggles to produce original content. The 70-30 Rule keeps you in check, helps you maintain a balance between your own Tweets and those from other people, while using the Retweet strategically.

I'm selective about who I Retweet, and like to alternate between Retweeting people who have lots of Followers and those who don't, but the key rule is that I want them to get maximum exposure on my Timeline, so that others Follow and Retweet them as well.

Okay, with that out of the way, this chapter will focus on the Strategic Retweet, and a few important ways in which you can use the Retweet to:

1. Gain specific kinds of Followers, such as journalists, VCs, bloggers, and professionals across various sectors.

2. Refresh/bring attention to older Tweets.

3. Encourage more people to Reply to your Tweets.

4. Get people who Follow Influencers to Follow you.

5. A Retweet that you will later undo, but which brings people to your Timeline.

1. Gain specific kinds of Followers: Suppose you want to get more bloggers to Follow you. You'll create a Private List called "Target Bloggers" and add 15-20 of the top bloggers that you want to Follow you to this List (they won't be notified as this is a Private List). Next:

1. Retweet one of the bloggers from your Target Bloggers List—pick someone that is likely to notice your Retweet. How do you determine this? Look at their Timeline--if they are actively replying to others, and Liking and Retweeting Tweets, they are likely to notice your effort. Make sure this Retweet remains at the top of your Twitter Timeline for at least four hours. Next:

   a. Like a few of the Tweets from other bloggers that are on your Target List. These could be colleagues and peers of the blogger you just Retweeted, and add them to a new Public List you will create called "Bloggers". If they have notifications turned on, they will notice this. Some will check out your Profile/Timeline, see that you have Retweeted one of their colleagues/peers, and may decide to Follow you. At the very least, you get them to notice you. Of course, some will wonder why you added them to a List instead of Liking and Following, when you've just Retweeted a fellow blogger, but this is exactly the thinking that pressures some into Following you first. If they Follow you first, that's a huge conversion of a Target, and you should Follow them back—although not immediately. Play it cool. Follow them in a few hours. See the Delayed Follow-back Rule for more.

   b. Review the last few Tweets of the blogger you just Retweeted to learn with whom they have recently interacted—other friends and colleagues. Visit the Twitter of these people, and "Deep Fave" (i.e. Like at least 6 Tweets on each Timeline) their Tweets. Follow one or two selectively. The ones you Followed may decide to Follow you back, after spotting a familiar face in your Timeline (the blogger you Retweeted), or after they notice that you are Following mutual friends.

   c. Review the Likes (click on the Likes tab on their Profile) of the blogger you just Retweeted, for additional clues into who they interact with—it's one way to find people who may have Mentioned the blogger you just Retweeted. Hop on to the Twitter Timeline of these (people who Mentioned the blogger) and Like a few of their Tweets, finding Tweets that contain multiple Twitter handles to maximize the impact of your Like.

d. Hop over to the blogger's Followers list. "Deep Fave" the Tweets of their last 50 Followers, including any Tweets that contain multiple Twitter handles—where the blogger's Followers are talking to other people.

e. Every two hours, Revisit the Timeline of the blogger you Retweeted, to check if they have posted new Tweets that include Replies or Mentions. Hop over to the Timelines of the people they have recently Mentioned or Replied to, and do the same as in 'a' above—i.e. Deep Fave their Tweets.

f. You can also search for Mentions of the blogger using Twitter's Search, and run the same Liking effort.

g. Move anyone that Follows you as a result of this maneuver from your Target List to the "Top Followers" Private List (as they no longer are a Target—you've converted them). Then, to satisfy the 70-30 Rule, you can Retweet them once a month or so, and

Try the above approach with VCs, journalists, photographers, brands, and others in your Target Lists. Do this every few days, and eventually you'll start to build a steady Following of people from your Target List, simply by using the Strategic Retweet.

2. Refresh/Bring attention to older Tweets: Retweet a great Reply that someone posted to one of your older Tweets (from a few hours/days earlier)—a Tweet that isn't visible in the First Four Tweets of your Timeline. This delayed Retweet refreshes your older Tweet, exposing it to a new set of people who probably missed it when it was originally posted. Upon seeing the Retweet in their Timeline, some will expand the details to Follow the conversation thread, and discover the original Tweet(s), which will result in more Retweets, Likes and Followers

a. Follow up this strategic Retweet by Liking the Tweets of the people with whom the person you Retweeted has recently interacted. Hop over to the Timeline of the person you Retweeted—then look at the last 15-20 Tweets they posted—and click on the handles of each of the people they had conversations with, to visit their Timelines. Like a few Tweets on each of the Timelines.

b. Next look at who recently Followed the person you just Retweeted, and Like a few of their Tweets

As a result of your actions in (a) and (b) above, if these friends of the person you Retweeted happened to have notifications turned on, they will likely visit your Profile, and when they notice that you have recently Retweeted someone they Follow or know, they are likely to Follow you as well—at the least, your "digital poke" has made them aware of your existence.

3. Encourage more people to Reply to your Tweets: Retweeting a smart Reply/Comment someone posted in response to your Tweet encourages others to join the conversation. This results in more Mentions of you on their Timeline, which results in more people visiting your Profile. Some of them might convert into Followers.

a. Retweet a Reply to your Tweet from a major influencer. Aside from a good humblebrag, this allows you to win over Followers of the Influencer when you Like their Tweets, using this approach.

b. Retweet a Reply that includes a major Influencer. For example, if one of your Tweets was Retweeted by someone with 100,000+ Followers, and one of their Followers replied to you via the Influencer's Retweet, this Reply will include your handle and the Influencer's handle. Retweet that Reply, because when people see that in their Newsfeed or on your Timeline, it signals to them that the Influencer Retweeted you. Upon expansion of the Reply, they'll see the original Tweet that was Retweeted by the Influencer, and this could lead to more Retweets of that Tweet, plus encourage people who Follow that Influencer to start Following you as well.

c. Alternate between Retweeting thoughtful Replies from people with both high follower and low follower counts. When people with low Follower counts see you Retweeting others with low Follower counts, it encourages them to Follow you and thoughtfully Reply to your Tweets.

4. Get people who Follow Influencers or who have recently interacted with Influencers to Follow you: If an Influencer has recently Mentioned you (perhaps to invite you to an event, complimented an article you wrote or a talk you gave), Retweet that Mention, and make sure that Retweet stays at the top of your Timeline for at least four hours. Then:

   a. Review the last few Tweets of the Influencer you just Retweeted to learn with whom they have recently interacted—other friends and colleagues. Visit the Twitter of these people, and "Deep Fave" (i.e. Like at least 6 Tweets on each Timeline) their Tweets. Follow one or two selectively.

   b. Review the Likes (click on the Likes tab on their Profile) of the Influencer you just Retweeted, for additional clues into who they interact with—it's one way to find people who may have Mentioned the Influencer you just Retweeted. Hop on to the Twitter Timeline of these (people who Mentioned the Influencer) and Like a few of their Tweets, finding Tweets that contain multiple Twitter handles to maximize the impact of your Like.

   c. Hop over to the Influencer's Followers list. "Deep Fave" the Tweets of their last 50 Followers, including any Tweets that contain multiple Twitter handles—where the Influencer's Followers are talking to other people.

   d. Every two hours, Revisit the Timeline of the Influencer whose Mention you Retweeted, to check if they have posted new Tweets that include Replies or Mentions of other people. Hop over to the Timelines of the people they have Mentioned or Replied to, and do the same as in 'a' above—i.e. Deep Fave their Tweets.

   e. Search for Mentions of the blogger using Twitter's Search, and run the same Liking effort.

What does all this result in? Well, when these people visit your Timeline, as a result of your Likes, and notice that one of the Influencers they Follow has Mentioned you, they are likely to Follow you as well. Using this approach, I added over 50 Followers from a single Retweet that mentioned me.

It is important that you let that Influencer Mention remain in your First Four Tweets for at least a few hours, to allow for people who don't actively check their Notifications to make the connection between your Like and the fact that you also Retweeted one of the Influencers they Follow.

Plus, any new people coming to your Timeline as a result of other referrals (not related to the Influencer Mention) will likely be impressed by that Mention, and also decide to Follow you.

5. A Retweet that you will later Undo: Sometimes you may need to Retweet a breaking news story, which will bring some of your Followers to your Timeline, where they can catch up with some of your other Tweets. Once a day or so has passed, that Tweet is no longer as important, so it would be okay to undo the Retweet. Best to choose a Tweet from a corporate news account (like @CNN) rather than from one of your Followers or someone you Follow, who might get offended about getting un-Retweeted.

When You Get a Big Retweet

It's going to happen, maybe even into Week 1 of applying these strategies—one of your Tweets will take off, and it'll get a crazy number of Retweets, which presents the perfect opportunity to add more Followers. How many Retweets that hot Tweet gets, plus how many new Followers you get as a result of your new exposure, depends on whether prospective new Followers are impressed by two things: your Bio and Timeline.

This is where obeying the 70-30 Rule can make the difference between getting a few vs. a lot of Followers. (Refer to the Bio, Groomed Timeline, and 70-30 Rule chapters.)

1. Do not Tweet for an hour. Chill for a bit. You want the Tweet to remain at the top of your Timeline and soak up as many

Retweets, Likes and Mentions as possible. Another good reason for holding that Tweet up at the top of your Timeline is to protect against Manual Retweeters (refer to the How to Deal with Manual Retweeters section).

2. Pin your best, most popular, or important Tweet (one that has the most Retweets, a celebrity Mention, or a Tweet that is especially significant to your work) to the top of your Timeline. As noted earlier, only those accessing Twitter via a desktop browser can see the Pinned Tweet—this feature is not available on mobile.

3. Groom your Timeline. Delete weird, useless Tweets if necessary to achieve the balance as outlined in the 70-30 Rule.

4. Keep a track of who all are Retweeting and Liking—a spreadsheet would be useful—for later analysis. You want to try to identify whose Retweet (I like to call these the Referring Retweet) is getting you those big Retweets. A quick way to tell this is by looking at the Notifications screen. When a Big Account (henceforth "Big Retweeter") with lots of engaged Followers Retweets you, your Notifications will explode. It will be like the Fourth of July of Retweets. You'll have to move quickly to figure out who that Big Retweeter was by looking at the list of Retweeters (click on the number of Retweets to see this list). If you don't move fast enough, you could misidentify the source of the big Retweet, plus, if the Tweet gets lots of Retweets, it could quickly remove the Big Retweeter from the list (Twitter, by default shows you only the last 25 Retweeters in Desktop and the last 100 in the mobile app). While this sounds like a high-class problem, you're losing vital intel by not moving fast and identifying the Big Retweeter(s). Why should you identify them? To add them to your Target List (Private List) if they don't already Follow you, and convert them.

   Add the ones that you think really helped set the Tweet on fire, including the ones that preceded the Big Retweeter—in many cases, it is the low-Follower accounts that catch the attention of the Big Retweeter(s).

5. Like any Comments and Replies to the Tweet that is getting the massive number of Retweets, to let people know you are engaged and listening, but don't reply to Comments, because you want that Tweet to remain at the top of your Timeline for at least a full hour, to soak up as many Retweets as it can. Make

an exception, however, for anyone seeking an important clarification that could further boost the Tweet. For example, if someone from a news organization is seeking permission to use your Tweet or a photo contained in that Tweet in a story.

6. After an hour has passed, pick a Reply that includes a major Influencer, and Retweet it. For example, if the Tweet was Retweeted by someone with 100,000+ Followers, and one of their Followers replied to the Retweet, their Reply will include your handle and the Influencer's handle. Retweet that Reply, because when people see that in their Newsfeed or on your Timeline, it signals to them that the Influencer Retweeted you, and this could lead to more Retweets of that Tweet, plus encourage people who Follow that Influencer to start Following you as well.

7. Like Tweets from people in your Lists:

    a. Like the Tweets of people from (Private) Target Lists (these are people that you want to Follow you back). If they have notifications turned on, they will hop over to your Timeline to see what's up. When they see that your last Tweet got mad action, plus that a major Influencer Retweeted you, they might decide to Follow you.

    b. Like the Tweets of people from your (Private) Like People and Top People Lists.

8. Search for and Like recent Tweets that match the keywords in your Tweet, to bring people who posted those Tweets to your Timeline.

9. Direct Message some of your old time Followers (but not the ones who just started Following you as a result of the big Retweet) to say hello, especially those that you have not interacted with in a while. This usually brings them to your Timeline, and if the Tweet is relevant or interesting enough to them, they might Retweet it.

10. After a couple of hours have passed, and the hot Tweet has accumulated an impressive number of Retweets, Retweet someone from your Target List. If this is a journalist, for example, Retweet them and then Follow a couple of other journalists, plus a couple of people from your Target Lists (make sure these people were recently active on Twitter, so you know

they'll notice your Follow). Like their Tweets. If these people have notifications turned on, they will hop over to your Timeline to see what's up. When they see that your last Tweet got mad action, and that you have Retweeted a fellow journalist, they might decide to Follow you back.

11. What you are saying by these efforts is, I got this awesome Tweet that is getting a lot of attention—people are Following me as a result. I have given someone (the journalist) exposure on my Timeline, so you may want to Follow me too.

12. Not all who Retweet you will Follow you, no matter how impressive you believe your Tweet was. How many Followers you get from a Big Retweet depends on:

    a. The state of your Bio and Timeline (refer to the "70-30" and the "First Four" Rules). If you got a 1000 Retweets, but only 20 new Followers, the only conclusion to draw is that your Timeline did not convince people you were worth a Follow.

    b. Who is Retweeting you and how long your Tweet remains on their Timeline (especially in the "First Four" position). The longer your Tweet remains in the First Four on the Timeline of a Big Account with lots of engaged Followers, better your chances of attracting new Followers.

    c. How you engage with the people who are Retweeting but not immediately Following: Remember, since I recommend that you do not Tweet for a few hours Following a Big Retweet (to allow the hot Tweet to remain at the top of your Timeline, defend against Manual Retweeters, and soak up as many Retweets as possible—see "1" above), your only option is to passively engage the people who are Retweeting:

        i. Hop over to their Timeline and "Deep Fave" (Like at least 6) their Tweets.

        ii. Add them to a Public List that makes it clear you are interested in them.

        iii. Like any Replies they post to your Tweet.

        iv. Selectively Follow some.

If they have notifications turned on, your efforts will be rewarded with a Follow.

As for the ones that still do not Follow you back but are attractive enough for you to try and gain as Followers, add them to a Private Target List, and use the steps outlined earlier fro converting Targets into Followers.

Retweet Multiple Tweets by Nesting/Categorizing Tweets

Ever wish you could multiple Tweets Retweeted with a single Retweet? Well, you can, simply by Replying to an older Tweet (let's call this the "Parent Tweet"), and stripping out your handle from the Reply. This is especially useful if you tend to Tweet about a handful of themes, and need to categorize similar Tweets (you can use any categorization system you want, I tend to rely on memory). By using Nested Tweets to string together related thoughts, even if those were Tweeted days or weeks apart, not only can you refresh old Tweets, but you can also boost Retweets on an old Tweet by 100% - 3000%. This is a better alternative to repeatedly posting a good Tweet.

Key things to remember about Nested Tweets:

1. When you Reply to an older ("Parent") Tweet, only existing Followers will see both the old and new ("Children") Tweets in their Newsfeed. However, when the Parent Tweet gets Retweeted, and people come to your Timeline after clicking through, they'll see only the new Child Tweet at the top of your Timeline, not the Parent Tweet, unless they expand the new Child Tweet. If the new Tweet is related and high quality, both the Parent (older Tweet) and Child (new) Tweet could get Retweeted by people seeing these Tweets for the first time.

2. If any of the Nested (Children) Tweets gets Retweeted, technically all Tweets in that chain can potentially gain exposure when people expand the Tweet details (scroll up or down from that Tweet), to review Replies/Comments. So a single Retweet can result in exposure for all Nested (Children) Tweets.

3. You can nest as many Tweets as you want, however, Twitter displays a maximum of three in your Followers' Newsfeed. So you if you've already Replied three times to a Tweet and nested a Tweet under the fourth Tweet, Twitter will display the first Tweet in the chain, the fourth Tweet you replied to, and the newest Tweet.

4. If you Nest Tweets often enough, you'll condition your Followers to scroll up and down through your Tweets to see if there are any 'Easter Egg' Tweets they missed. When they find those, some might get Retweeted, Liked or commented upon.

5. Try to not overdo this, as it can become annoying, and vary the timing (look at the timestamps of the Parent Tweets) to avoid overexposing people to the same Tweets.

Also, try keeping old, but great, Tweets alive by posting them on LinkedIn. I've had several old Tweets Retweeted by using this approach.

Defend against Manual Retweets

It's inevitable. Some Big Account with tens of thousands of Followers will decide to do a Manual Retweet of one of your hot Tweets from two weeks ago—a Tweet that is likely no longer present in the Last Twenty Tweets. And now your Mentions are blowing up because people are Retweeting the Manual RT, likely because they came to your Profile and couldn't find that Tweet. This could be frustrating because this Manual Retweet sucked Retweets from your original Tweet.

On the other hand, you should be grateful that you're getting partial credit because the Manual Retweeter decided to include your @handle in the Manual RT, instead of outright stealing your Tweet. And you also likely got a few new Followers as a result of that exposure.

So here's couple of ways in which you can score back some of those Retweets. The key here is to make it easy for people who come to your Profile to see evidence of that old Tweet almost immediately, so they can Retweet it directly.

1. First, pull up your original Tweet that just got Manually Retweeted by running a search on Twitter, using your handle and some of the keywords in that Tweet.

   Qupte that Tweet or just Retweet it to bump it up to the top of your timeline so it becomes the first one that people see.

2. See who all are Retweeting and liking your Manual Retweet, and Like their Tweets. If this brings them back to your Profile, they'll see your Quoted/Retweeted Tweet, and may end up Retweeting it.

Reward People who Retweet

One of the best ways to reward loyal followers is to Retweet them.

1. Anyone that Follows you and Retweets and Likes frequently is obviously looking to be rewarded in kind. Hop over to their Timeline and do the due diligence (they are real, not a bot, are not racist, sexist, etc.), and if you sense they are genuinely trying to build a real relationship, Follow them back.

2. Retweet one of their good Tweets, instead of just Tweeting out a "thank you"—or if you can't find a good Tweet after an intensive examination of their Timeline, Retweet one of their good replies to your Tweets.

4. Add them to your "Like People" and "Retweeted Me" Private Lists, so you can Like their Tweets on a frequent basis, and Retweet them periodically.

5. Engage them in conversations—Direct Message them periodically to say how much you appreciate their Tweets. Take a genuine interest—mention a Tweet of theirs that you particularly liked.

Dealing with Un-Followers

1. If you Follow someone, and later learn that they have un-Followed you, Like a few of their Tweets, and if they Follow you back again, the un-Follow was likely accidental.

2. If they don't Follow you back within a couple of days, un-Follow them.

3. Add them to a Private List called "Un-Followers" if you want to keep a record of these people.

4. Block and Report accounts that you believe are using the Follow/Un-Follow tactic to get attention.

Take a "Break"

You'll have some terrible days on Twitter, with dud Tweets. Delete those, if that makes you feel better. Take a break for a few days. But if you can't make it a complete break, do this: Stop Tweeting, and turn to listening and organizing.

1. A break from Tweeting allows for the Tweets on your Timeline to soak up some Likes and Retweets—not a bad deal.

2. Use the break to catch up on Tweets you may have missed. Read and Like the Tweets from your various Lists. Organize people into Lists. Find new people to Follow. Convert people in your Target lists into Followers. Direct Message and Retweet (use 70-30 Rule) people with a low follower count to encourage them. Listening and observing has helped me better understand the rhythm of my Twitter universe.

3. Take notes—who had a great Tweet? What topics are trending? What was the best treatment you saw of a particular story? Why? These notes might inspire your next great Tweet.

4. Review your last few Tweets and analyze what you could have done better. How do those compare to your best Tweets?

The Key Takeaways

A quick summary of the most important things we covered in this book:

1. <u>Bio, Profile and Cover Picture</u>: You get <u>10 seconds and the first four tweets</u> on your Timeline to convince someone to Follow you. How to optimize your Bio and Timeline for these critical 10 seconds, and convert first-time Visitors into Followers<u>Groomed Timeline</u>: 70-30 Rule--70% of Tweets in your Timeline should be yours, 30% Retweets—to increase your odds of being Followed. Pay particular attention to the First Four Tweets:

   a. First Four "above the fold" Tweets in your Timeline (as viewed on Mobile): Quality of these Tweets largely determines whether people will follow you. Make sure these Tweets are positive, helpful, offer a unique POV and that at least one includes a visual. Ideal composition of the First Four Tweets:

      i. One Retweet

      ii. One Reply

      iii. Two original thoughts

         1. Related to profession/industry

         2. Not related to profession/industry

   b. Overall Timeline:

      i. <u>Not to chatty</u>: 1-2 Tweets at the most per conversation thread (always insert the message before the handle). No more than 1-2 quality Tweets if live-Tweeting Conferences and joining Twitter Chats. Aim for no more than 8-10 quality Tweets per day (including Replies and Retweets), or you could get Muted or un-Followed.

      ii. Visually striking: Timeline at-a-glance should immediately convey that you are a confident Retweeter. Make good, but not excessive, use of visuals.

    iii. Retweet people with high and low Follower counts.

    iv. <u>Maintain diversity of thought in your Timeline</u>: Tweet about more than one theme and let your Retweets also indicate your support for variety.

    v. Healthy engagement: Ultimate proof is in the Retweets, Likes and Replies. Engage with others, and they'll return the favor.

    vi. Limit use of hashtags and links within Tweets.

    vii. Delete automated Tweets: Horoscopes, fitness app posts, Follower/Unfollower stats, Swarm app check-ins, Meerkat/Periscope tweets.

    viii. Delete racist, sexist or otherwise unhelpful Tweets.

2. <u>Aesthetic of each Tweet</u> matters:

    a. Shorter is better: 80-100 characters.

    b. Overlay narrative on to a visual if you need more space for your message.

    c. Always seek a unique angle: Search for how others have treated that topic, and find a better angle.

    d. Use humor when possible.

    e. When Replying, <u>insert message before handles</u>.

3. <u>Like Frequently</u>: For every 1 Tweet, Like 100 Tweets of others, paying particular attention to people in your Like People and Target Lists.

4. <u>Join conversations</u> to get your content noticed and shared, instead of posting a standalone Tweet (which might not get noticed). Search for conversations already taking place related to a particular topic that you want to Tweet about, and insert what you meant to Tweet into the conversation.

5. Don't Tweet a lot after a big Retweet. Allow it to soak up as many Retweets as possible. Strategically use "Digital Pokes"—Direct Messages, Likes, Add-to-Lists, and Follows to get people to visit your Timeline, especially after you post a Tweet and get a big Retweet.

6. Use Private and Public Lists to make it easy to engage with people you are Following and your Followers, and to convert Targets (people you want to Follow you) into Followers.

7. Retweet yourself: Bump/refresh old Tweets using delayed Retweet and delayed Reply, plus Nesting/Replying to old Tweets.

8. Analyze everything and learn from every Tweet (who Retweets and Likes you, the big Retweeters, the non-interacting/passive Followers). Observe and learn from what others are getting right too.

9. Take a Break when you're running out of inspiration or feeling overwhelmed.

10. Always be:

    a. Encouraging and rewarding your best followers: Like generously according to the 1-100 Rule. Retweet according to the 70-30 Rule.
    b. Building an audience: Include your Twitter handle in emails, on name badges, and on other social networks.

Conclusion

I sincerely believe that if you can master how to build an audience on Twitter, the opportunities are endless, particularly if you harness the power of Twitter for the collective benefit of sharing human knowledge.

I do look forward to your feedback, especially any hacks that you may have discovered.

To send me your comments, just follow me at @Khanoisseur and @hackthebird, and Direct Message me. I'll feature the best responses on my Twitter accounts.